FRANCIS FOR MEN

'Otherwise, We Need Weapons'

MARKUS HOFER

Translated by Sharon Therese Nemeth
Foreword by Richard Rohr, O.F.M.

ST. ANTHONY MESSENGER PRESS

Cincinnati, Ohio

Cover and book design by Mark Sullivan
Cover includes an image by Gene Plaisted, O.S.C.

This book was first published in German, as *Franz für Männer,*
copyright ©2001, Tyrolia-Verlag, Innsbruck-Vienna

CONTENTS

FOREWORD

It is important that Markus Hofer decided to write a book about Francis of Assisi, and even more important that it is a book not about Francis as a saint—which he also is—but about Francis as a man; not as an ideal of something, or a figure of protest against something, but as an ordinary man who had to embark on his human journey, to take his own path in life, just as every person must do. In rightfully choosing to view Francis as an "Everyman" the author discovered an archetype.

Viewed in this way, Francis may be seen to have united many elements into his one original self. As a man he had both the qualities of a masculine knight and a feminine poet; he could love women as well as men in a deep and caring way. He was a man who trusted God instinctually at a time when no one recognized the church, who trusted God even when everything he heard about God seemed to be falling apart, a man who battled with his sexuality and transformed it creatively, a man who raised fundamental questions about institutionalized forms of religion and culture, a man who could be just as fanatical as he was flexible, a man who took political action by living out the gospel of Jesus in the most radical way, a man of the church in a way that was completely focused on creation. He was a man who has been a figurehead for ecology, a church reformer, a peacemaker, a multitalented artist, a role model for the ecumenical movement as well as for those seeking a simpler way of life. He is an example for all forms of brotherly love, for defenders of animal rights, for astronomers and dreamers, for holy fools, for beggars and he is even a prototype for the Italian male. This one-of-a-kind man did a lot of things right! He is justifiably considered to be "the greatest natural spiritual genius of the West." He has been written about so frequently that in the library of international languages he has the single longest bibliography. He is treasured in cultures around the world. And Assisi was the Christian city where the pope could imagine inviting the leading heads of world religion.

But Francis' renown does not have so much to do with his carrying out his actions in a perfect way—because he was not a systematic thinker, his actions did not always make sense and he also made some significant mistakes. If we look at Francis honestly, it seems he had a few pretty outrageous ideas, and it's easy to imagine that it would not have been completely easy to live with him. He was judgmental, demanding, self-important, petty, inconsistent and had an oversized ego. He behaved like a conceited teenager toward his father, treated his brothers like children and Clare as if she were a seductress. He loved dramatic gestures that placed him in the center of attention. One time just for fun we even called him the "Patron of Exhibitionists"! Whatever the case may be, he had a deep-seated need to be someone special. From a contemporary point of view, we can't say with certainty whether he always sensed things more deeply or was sometimes just being a cheap sentimentalist. In my opinion he was not only great in life, but also great in sin—in other words: he had a calling. Those who have a calling are the people who are needed by God. They hold a lot together because they are held together by a mighty love. They are living icons of this integral process that we call conversion or enlightenment.

Francis held all of the colors of life together and thus was as radiant as the whiteness of the sun. Darkness was not left out of him, but rather in him was embraced, reconciled and transformed into a new kind of light. He held the different elements suspended and balanced them against or with each other so that the result was pure art and poetry. He held the center, the middle, so tightly—or, more accurately, he let himself be held by God so tightly—that all these parts joined together, fused with each other and created something truly new. He blended forgiveness into fanaticism; he balanced self-importance with mild goodness and with his great soul the feelings of sentimentality. He brought God and man into harmony, because it was exactly in this union that he was able to recognize Jesus as his role model. In his soul he united human will and grace, his intentions and his gifts because he saw God did the same with him. He maintained the balance between his masculine and feminine sides and also between the sides of him that were adult and childlike, and he did this in such a way that was only possible because another was working in him. It was another who let him be counted, who loved him, who forgave him, who accepted him and freed him in such a profound way that he could finally do the same for himself, for others and maybe for us all. He held much together because he finally allowed God to hold him together.

Whatever enlightenment is, it does not seem like something we can achieve by ourselves. Rather, it is always given to us and happens to us. It is like a high wire act in which great daring and trust are pre-conditions. It is less an act of perfection than an act of letting go. It is less a question of performance and reward than an act of trusting love. It has less to do with the continual fight between good and evil than opening the way for the flow of endless compassion for ourselves and others. And last but not least, enlightenment has to do with thankfulness—thankfulness and joy for what is. Religions call this holiness; for ordinary people it is just being human.

Father Richard Rohr, O.F.M.
Albuquerque, New Mexico

PREFACE

Saint Francis and me—this was not love at first sight. As the supposedly always kind and loving "Brother Happy," Saint Francis did not especially impress me. Then one day while visiting his hermitage in Tuscany something happened inside me. I discovered his unknown and indisputably wild sides. After that something also affected me as a man. In any case Saint Francis did not let go of me, and I did not let go of him. The first result was a comprehensive book about the historical figure of Francis of Assisi. The more I blew away the dust of the pious historical writings, the more striking and fascinating was the figure that emerged. When I finished the book I was not yet finished with him. As a man I continued to face this unique man. There was still more.

I undertook several trips with male groups to the wild locations of his hermitages, and we were all affected. Thoughts, feelings, sensations emerged that did not fit the scheme of my first book. Feelings and thoughts opened up for which I had to find a form, and when I came to write in the words of Saint Francis himself, my writing took the form of literary fiction. While writing, however, I had the feeling that these were things I must express. A flow evolved between my experience as an individual man, the male experience as a whole and that of this man from Assisi. I felt practically compelled to write *Francis for Men*.

This book did not turn out to be a pious book, but it is a spiritual one—at least, as I understand spirituality. Deep dimensions of what it means to be a man opened up, or, better said, flowed together with a view to Saint Francis, the man from Assisi. In this flowing river lay many things, not the least of which was my contact with Richard Rohr, O.F.M., whom I would like to thank at this time. Many men I have known were part of this flow: my father, my grandfather, mentors, friends and, of course, members of the Franciscan orders. I would like to dedicate this book to all of them. I have written it for men who want to understand themselves better, who sense that there is more to being a man than they have heretofore experienced, and that this new experience has fascinating dimensions. For us men life has its everchanging challenges, and this is just one reason why it is so suspenseful. If each reader of this book finds only one sentence with personal meaning, which strengthens or inspires change, then the writing of it has been worthwhile.

Women play only a small part here. When my wife read the manuscript for the first time, she was fascinated. She said: "If a woman wants to learn more about men, she should read this book. If she wants to find out something about women, she'll be disappointed." It is a book about men for men. But perhaps this is exactly what also makes it a book for women who are curious about men.

GIOVANNI DI PIETRO DI BERNARDONE

Giovanni, the son of Pietro di Bernardone, first saw the light of day, presumably, in winter at the beginning of the year 1182. Although winters in Assisi can be cold, there is seldom snowfall. If there is snow today, postcards are printed for the following year, with great pride in the thin layer of white splendor. When Giovanni came into the world—we know neither date of birth nor baptism—his father was away on a business trip in France. His father was a cloth merchant and the fashionable material from Provence in France was then the latest rage. In contrast to today, childbirth was exclusively a woman's domain, and as a man he probably would not even have been allowed into the birthing room. The father, later depicted as the bad guy of this story, would undoubtedly have flown home at the time of birth if a cell phone and airplane had been handy. He loved his firstborn son more than anything else and set all his hopes on him. But he was far away and his wife, Giovanni's mother, about whom we know almost nothing, had the baby baptized with this name. The absence of the father at the time of birth and Giovanni's later difficulties with him could lead to the hasty assumption that Giovanni was a soft mama's boy. However, we can say with certainty that it is not as simple as that, and later in life Giovanni showed just how much of the manly dynamism he had inherited from his father.

When Pietro di Bernardone returned to Assisi from his business trip, loaded down with fine cloth, he rechristened his son, and in his pride and happiness named him Francesco: little Francis, or just Francis as we call him today. Not that Pietro made an extra trip to the priest for that reason, apart from the fact that there was also not yet a patron saint with that name. On his baptismal certificate, if there was one, the name Giovanni di Pietro de Bernardone, or something similar, could probably still be read today. At that time there were hardly any fixed surnames, except among the nobility, and more often nicknames were used in order to tell all the Pietros and Giovannis apart.

SON OF THE NOUVEAU RICHE

Francis was the firstborn son of a newly rich family. His father was a respected resident of the city of Assisi and also belonged to a new social class. Up to that time there had only been two social classes: the nobility and the peasant class, the powerful and the weak, the rich and the poor. However, at this time the new and increasingly stronger class of the ambitious bourgeoisie emerged, with the economy to thank for their power. Through trade, industry and, above all, the market economy, the bourgeoisie gained in position, influence and more and more in political power as well. Against this backdrop a civil war broke out in Assisi when Francis was just sixteen years old. The nobility of the city was initially defeated and fled to Perugia.

As is so often the case, it is the children of the newly rich who act so truly nouveau riche, that is, ostentatiously flaunting their privilege and riches. It was still clear to the father how much hard work it took to earn money and how easily a streak of monetary good fortune could dry up. His social confidence as a prominent citizen was more likely to show itself in his inwardly proud attitude and less in his being surrounded with status symbols. His extroverted son, who considered excessively expensive clothing to be exactly the right ones, took over in this area. He was a clotheshorse with a weakness for fashionable clothing that could not be extravagant enough. Once, when the exquisiteness of the cloth could not be outshone any further, he sewed an old scrap of cloth onto the expensive garment to create an even trendier look.

Francis had a certain need to stand out, was not completely lacking in vanity and more than likely was something of a show-off as well. He was a person who liked to put himself on display, a trait that he probably retained all his life. We can imagine him as an average Central Italian male, not too tall, lively, full of energy, with twinkling eyes, a man who put into practice what he talked about, who spoke with his whole body, who gestured, who knew that a few show elements couldn't hurt anything and who understood a lot about dramatization. Francis must have made a great impact on people through his manner alone. His sermons, which were for the most part fairly standard, must have owed much of their remarkable effect to his delivery of them. The impression of the humble, bowed man conveyed in the famous painting by Cimabue is deceptive. Francis, however, was not merely a show-off but was very much loved by his contemporaries in Assisi because of his lighthearted and winning ways, not the least of which was his generosity. He not only spent his money on clothing but also in an almost wasteful manner on banquets. His parents scolded him because of this, but they did not stop him.

The dream of many young men in the up-and-coming bourgeois society was the life of a knight. Some even set their sights on the nobility. Francis had an undeniable weakness for this way of life, which was not only reflected in his aristocratic clothing but also in how he expressed himself and in his love of the French songs of the troubadours, at that time the latest craze. His father had brought back some of these songs from France with him, and even later in life, when he was happy and euphoric, Francis often switched to French and sang these songs.

THE APPLE AND ITS TREE

To the father it was clear that his son was to take over the cloth business, and he taught his son everything he needed to know to do this. Francis was in a school for only a short time and his Latin was more bad than good; he was presumably better at French. He was more likely to have learned the language skills he needed to write business documents, contracts and invoices. It is certain that his father, who involved him early in the business, had made sure of that.

This father was later depicted in the darkest of images. It is true that he could not understand his son's changes, but at the same time, Pietro was forced to bury all the hopes he had placed in his son. It is true that he was furious when his son simply sold off their most expensive fabrics for money, but Pietro had worked hard to earn the money to buy those fabrics in the first place. It is true that he was completely ashamed when his first-born turned up in Assisi, freezing, half-starved and in rags, but he was ashamed because he loved him more than anything else. But why did it still have to come to such a clash? Because two bullheaded men confronted each other. The characters of both men were not really so different as the first impression might suggest. The apple does not fall far from the tree, as the saying goes. Naturally, the son turned the meaning of this around completely, but constitutionally they were quite similar. Both were decisive and energetic men, consistent in their behavior, which is why things could not go on with the two of them. And both were ambitious. If it was important for one to become the richest man in Assisi, the other wanted, without question, to be the poorest of the poor. Both knew exactly what they wanted and it was exactly this quality that made them so similar.

Francis: I have to smile now, but this is actually something interesting. For me, the situation with my father was over and done with following what happened in front of the bishop's palace. It was absolutely clear to me what I had to do, and this was also not directed against my father as a person. Naturally he could have said the same thing himself. For him a whole world had fallen apart without question, this has become clear to me now. I almost feel sorry for him when I think about it.

Were we really so similar? I always just saw him as my opposite. For me he always remained the one who couldn't understand me, and who wanted to keep me from following my calling. But most likely I couldn't understand him either. We were both so convinced of our own objectives. And it's true that in this way we were exactly alike. But this still didn't help. I had to do what I did—and so did he. It seemed that things had to be as they were. Seen from the outside it's true that two stubborn men had a head-on confrontation. This perspective has something reconciliatory for me. I also have to allow my father the right I claimed for myself. The separation between us was necessary. It was unavoidable. I had to do things differently than he did. But is this a reason to put oneself above one's father?

Slowly I am able to let him be as he was, and the best part is that a comforting peace has come over me at the same time. How often do we sons want to change our fathers, and where do we get this idea? It's as if much later I could offer my hand to him in reconciliation. Maybe he was waiting longer than I was for something like that.

It's really not easy to admit that we were much more alike than it seemed on the surface. Later I never thought about my father much. He should just do what he wants, I thought. It's true that I had to separate myself from him, but that's no reason anyone should have felt compelled to make him into a villain or a scapegoat. That's also why it's hard to admit this now. If you look at it honestly, we had a lot in common. I might be the "great Francis," but at this moment as a son a feeling of humility and thankfulness toward my father comes over me.

A Young Man Dislocated

In the first civil war the nobility were defeated and many of them fled to the neighboring town of Perugia. Four years later there was a renewed war involving the cities of Assisi and Perugia, allied with the nobility of Assisi. It seemed the hour had come for the young aspiring knight. With his twenty years Francis entered the war between the cities on horseback and in the manner of a nobleman. But it was all to no avail. Assisi lost the Battle of Colestrada, and Francis was taken prisoner. The peace charter of 1202 renewed the rights of the nobility in the city, and citizens were forced to pay high reparations. Undoubtedly the cloth merchant Bernardone had to dig deeply into his pockets as well.

Francis sat in the Perugia prison for over a year, and it was at this time that the first small, quiet signs of his new story began to appear. He stood apart from his beaten-down comrades with a cheerfulness that seemed at times almost suspicious. They thought he was crazy, and it is in fact the story of a great craziness that began at this time, a craziness that continues to touch us today, that took shape gradually, one tug after the other until he had completely changed his direction. The greatest fool in the world, as he later called himself, still laughed when there was nothing left to laugh about. When one knight acted unjustly toward a fellow prisoner and was shunned by the others because of it, Francis was the only one who did not end a friendship with the knight.

Perhaps Francis already guessed that the right to change for the better would be taken away from the knight if he were alienated. In any case, the fool placed himself on the side of the scapegoat and did this out of an inexplicable but deeply sensed conviction. Because of this he was considered to be crazy by his comrades, but not a lost cause.

When he went off to this war at age twenty, Francis was a young entrepreneur through and through. It is true that he was not really a knight but a town citizen who also faced his opponents politically. What began now did not have anything more to do with post-pubescent bravado. If today in Italy men move out of "Hotel Mama" at the age of thirty on the average, it was different at that time. Even if Francis also lived at home and was single, he was without a doubt completely involved in his father's business as a young merchant who already shouldered his share of the responsibility. The story that begins here is one of a young man and not of a young professional turned rebel or the uninspired drifting of a soft mama's boy who does not know what to do if his mother does not tell him first. It is the story of a young man who senses, hears and acts.

After Francis was freed from prison, which again probably cost his father Pietro a pretty penny, he was beset with a long illness as a result of his one-year stay behind bars. He was certainly not a colossus physically nor was his health exceptionally robust. When a nobleman in the city was arming troops for a new campaign in Apulia, a fever of another kind burned within him. Francis was caught up in the new chance to become a knight and equipped himself, at least at first, as he saw fit. The young Assisi citizen and would-be knight arrived equipped like a dandy with armor even more elaborate than that of the nobleman, who was not exactly destitute. The evening before they were to set off, another small tug revealed itself when he gave away his expensive attire to a third party: a poor knight who also wanted to join them but could not afford a proper suit of armor.

The following night Francis dreamt about a grand palace filled with splendid armaments. The voice in the dream announced that this palace belonged to him and his knights. In the dream he recognized that something great would become of him. He was sure of this the next morning, when he saw his destiny as a great emperor, which spurred him on with even greater joy and eagerness toward the campaign.

From Assisi the broad valley draws toward the south, where it narrows after approximately a day's ride to Spoleto. This is where the first rest was made, and in the early night another dream brought another revelation that forced the dreamer to make a correction. It seemed he had misunderstood the dream of the night before, evident now in the voice asking him if he wished to serve the servant or the Lord. He recognized that it was the Lord himself speaking to him and was prepared to do what was asked of him. He thought he should return to Assisi and that he would find out there what to do. Sleep was impossible the rest of the night, and on the following day Francis returned to his hometown. Nothing remained of the hoped-for knighthood.

Francis: Was I a dreamer? To a modern-day man I'm sure it seems that way, and this was in fact a part of it. For many I became a dreamer in the true sense of the word when I began to put into action what the dream had told me. It wasn't so easy to explain when I returned home two days after the campaign had begun. As you might think I was the subject of more than a little ridicule, but the dream made it worthwhile in spite of everything.

We dream a lot, and often our dreams seem like emotional processing plants. But on these two nights there was something different about my dreams. That's why I was able to describe them in such detail. It was suddenly so clear to me that no more questions remained. I knew I had a special calling—that was crystal clear to me—even if I was a long way from being conscious of what it was. It's so hard to put into words and it probably sounds like bragging again, but I sensed a certainty and deep conviction inside me. I had no choice—otherwise I would have betrayed myself. It isn't easy when you don't know something for sure and nobody can explain it. It might be called a full-blown illusion, but for me it was a question of whether or not I was being true to myself. The dream was a part of me and a part of my own clarity.

On the second night I was aware that it was the Lord God himself who spoke to me. I know how dangerous such statements can be, even more so today than at that time. Maybe God doesn't speak to you anymore because you don't think he will. How do all the people who have drawn in their antennas expect to receive anything? Normally it doesn't hit you like a bolt of lightning as it did Saint Paul, who had his life-changing experience on the way to Damascus. In fact it would be better if things didn't get that far. It isn't seldom that a lightning bolt hits men today in the form of a heart attack or another misfortune, and then they still don't get it. A lightning bolt always means you have to change your life. But one thing I want to make clear is that the dream was my dream. You can't base your life on my dream. I don't know what your path is, and it doesn't have to be the same as mine. And you certainly shouldn't all become Franciscans on account of me! I'm happy if I can reach just one of you because I followed my dream and went my way without compromise. It's only bad when you stop asking questions, stop listening, let your antennae rust, believing that you know everything and that you know it all better, and when you stop expecting him. Then you'll waste away and never know the greatness he has in store for you. And when you sense it and hear it, then act on it as well.

THE KNIGHT CHANGES HIS BRIDE

At first Francis simply returned to his previous life and became, with his twenty-three years, the designated ringleader of the youth again, a sort of king for a day, who often picked up the tab for diverse festivities. Well known for his big-hearted nature, Francis seemed to have been an obvious choice for this role. As they were making their way through the streets of Assisi one night, perhaps a little drunk, he suddenly stopped in his tracks with a look of transfiguration on his face. Some would have asked themselves if he had downed one too many drinks. Others might have thought he had fallen in love and told him to own up. Yes, he was to take a bride, Francis said, but one who was nobler, richer and more beautiful than any they had ever seen. This information satisfied the nighttime party animals. In his ecstasy—for Francis was an ecstatic person and we can count on further such incidents in his story—the next tug was felt.

One of the greatest duties of a medieval knight was to serve a bride, or lady-love. This was something that applied to a knight even if his chances for success were minimal. In addition to withstanding perilous adventure, the expression of courtly love was simply one of the fundamental duties of knighthood. On this particular night the passions of the would-be knight received a new sense of meaning. It became clear to him, once again dramatically, that poverty was the bride in whose service he would enter as a knight. In his courtly metaphorical language, poverty was the noble bride who wedded herself to the young knight and whom he wanted to serve in the future. It was consequently the poor begging for alms who profited most from his generosity from then on. There was still much infatuation and bliss involved. The way his path would continue was still anything but clear, although he had found his focus: poverty. But what should he do with it now? Francis tried and experimented, sometimes in quite a blundering and awkward manner, but he did not give up.

When he was twenty-four Francis arrived in Rome during a pilgrim journey. Full of indiscriminate enthusiasm he was annoyed at how little people donated at the tombs of the apostles, and with a resounding clatter threw his entire reserve of silver coins before the altar, an action that did not fail to have its effect on the astonished bystanders. When he came out of the church he saw the poor begging for alms. He asked one of them to lend him his rags, which he exchanged for his designer clothes, and began begging for alms in French. The refined merchant's son dressed in borrowed rags and begging in his elegant French must have been quite a sight. We can assume he noticed this himself, for he put his own clothes back on again, returned the rags and went home to Assisi. There he turned to the Lord and asked God to show him the way he should take. This way did not yet seem to be quite the right one.

Bride Poverty, the image borrowed from knighthood, was his ideal, but it was still one he cultivated from the safe distance of a bourgeois existence. He was still the well-off almsgiver with the emotional backup of his protected existence. Keeping with this metaphor—the marriage was still not consecrated. It still could have been seen as the romantic eccentricity of an idealistic merchant's son. However, the wedding came sooner than he expected, and it came differently than he imagined. The bride confronted him in the most awful reality and awaited her wedding kiss.

One day in the valley below the city he encountered a leper. Up to now this sight had been so disgusting that he had to look away every time, and the smell was so horrible that he always held his nose. This scene—just to let it sink in for a minute—although not the last, was the final decisive tug that transformed him inwardly. More attractive and more pious scenes were later deemed the de facto event, but it was this wedding kiss that opened the gate to his own path, a gate that at the same time immediately closed behind him.

The leper reached out his hand to him. Francis gave him alms and kissed his hand. The disfigured face looked at him and the leper lifted his hands for the kiss of peace. This would have been the last chance to run away and there would have been reason enough to do so. Francis embraced the leper, whose sores were oozing with pus, and kissed him. And in doing so the gate closed behind him. Indeed, although he got back on his horse and rode away, he did not really go back anymore.

To return to the previous imagery: now he was married. Some would say in mockery that it must have been a great wedding night! And it was, if in a completely different sense from the usual. Even in his final *Testament* Francis spoke about this scene: *what seemed to me as bitter was transformed into sweetness of the soul and the body*. After this event nothing was as it had been before, and he was also no longer the same. He left the scene, defying all expectation, in a state of unimaginable exuberance. It was not the pride of a particularly Christian knight who had done a valiant social deed. The previous images break down at this point. Something had changed inside him, something that could be sensed physically—not as pride in his chest but as unexpected butterflies in his stomach. A warmth and strength radiated from this embrace, something that he could not yet easily put into words. It was a feeling of elation that changed him and his world once and for all. He was happy.

Francis: *Later I even ate out of the same bowl as a leper
who had festering sores. But it is exactly these unattrac-
tive and repulsive images that are unimportant. The
crazy part was what happened afterward: I was happi-
er than I had ever been up to that time and, more importantly, in a way I didn't even know existed. At the same
time I had the feeling that this was not my doing, that
this was not any kind of special achievement. I would
not have traded what I felt afterward for anything in the
world. The words I used then were right on target and I
can't do any better today: what seemed to me as bitter
became sweet. Therefore it was simply magnificent and
unexplainable at the same time. I was happy, cheerful
and lighthearted in a way that I never could have imagined possible before. There is nothing more I can tell you
about it.*

*But I can tell you more about the time before. Lepers
repulsed me, in fact more than I can put into words.
Every time I saw one my throat and stomach tightened
up and I could have thrown up. I felt sorry for them, of
course, as long as they were banned from the town.
Thank God, I would have said, because I didn't have to
see them, and then felt guilty about it afterward, like
you're supposed to. You know how it is. But I just couldn't
help always making a detour around them.*

*However, it probably has less to do with the lepers
themselves. They are just the concrete example in my
case. All of you have your "lepers," probably less shock-
ing than in my day, things that you constantly avoid, that
you continually make a detour around. The interesting
part is that these "lepers" don't disappear because you*

avoid them. They appear beyond the next curve in the road again, and you always need an incredible amount of energy to avoid them. They can be the realities of your life—people, relationships, feelings and so on. They control your life without your wanting them to or admitting that they do. It costs you all of your energy to avoid them. And when you sweep them under the carpet they don't just stay there, or, at the very least, you trip over them time after time. Maybe you know what I mean.

Though it's all very well for me to talk about it today, the solution is simple. Solutions look a lot easier after the fact, or when you're on the outside looking in. You can run away from your "lepers" as long as you want. They will always catch up to you. You can fight, repress, ignore or restrain them as much as you want, and it won't do any good. You have to confront them. In life there is sometimes no getting past or around something, and then the only approach must be through it. You have to embrace your lepers. This is the only act that helps.

IN THE BELLY OF THE WHALE

It was a kiss without a return ticket. The path lay before him; the gate behind him had already closed shut. A way back into the bourgeoisie existence of a merchant's son was no longer possible. He was married, already given away to Bride Poverty. Self-confident as he was—in fact he had the deepest conviction he would accomplish something great—he still had no idea what it would be. The path lay before him but he did not have much more than a vague orientation. There was more fog than clarity, more bewilderment than signposts. He must have made this impression on the people in Assisi as well. When it came down to it, he would have loved to have shared what had happened, but he wanted to keep a low profile. When this proved impossible he ended up bewildering everyone. Be that as it may, he also had to explain why he was not in Apulia. More than a few would have shaken their heads about this fool. At this time he was probably the biggest mystery to himself.

After the embrace of the leper, Francis wandered around, mostly outside the city walls, and he could often be found in a small, dilapidated chapel below where the city descended to the plains. In those days the chapel was a peaceful place of escape, far away from the commotion of the city, where everyone knew him and he was approached again and again. And so one day he entered the ramshackle little church of San Damiano, which was seldom visited except by the impoverished priest who looked after it. It was a plain, long, black, sooty building, the roof no longer watertight and the masonry neglected and crumbling. A simple, Romanesque cross hung over the altar, more than likely the only bright spot in the little church.

Somehow Francis was not able to walk past the chapel without going inside. Filled with high spirits and helplessness at the same time, he was constantly in search of a signpost to give him a clear direction. He simply wanted to know what he must do. In such situations there is presumably nothing that happens by chance. Francis entered the chapel, began to pray before the cross and received his directive: *Don't you see how my house has fallen into disrepair? Therefore, go and rebuild it again.* Francis was no philosopher who brooded a long time over such a directive. He now knew what he must do, and things just took their course from there.

But something else changed during the time he remained in the chapel. Up to now he had stuck by the image of the knight and his bride, which had gained a new meaning with the embrace of the leper. But where should the knight get his instructions and whose knight should he be? Where was his round table? Even when he had declared himself a knight of poverty, with much inner fanfare, the image was not enough to give him the strength he needed. But the new image was visibly before him: the crucified Christ. It is the image of the Son of God who placed himself on the side of all who are crucified and enslaved and in doing so was forced to endure the greatest suffering himself. The way Francis identified himself with the crucified Christ is one we can only comprehend with difficulty— until he receives the stigmata on La Verna.

This new image dislocated him entirely and now he knew no limits. Francis was a man for whom there was only either/or. In this sense he was radical in a way that was almost frightening. If Christ suffered, then he must also suffer. Without mercy he castigated his own body and did not indulge himself in any way. His later warning to the brothers against excessive fasting was something he never applied to himself. He was hard and uncompromising toward himself in a way that he never expected of anyone else. As much as all of nature was brother and sister to him, his own body, "Brother Ass" as he called it, must be broken. Yet on his deathbed Francis had to confess that he had sinned much against Brother Ass.

But back to the events that followed his experience with the image of the cross in San Damiano and led to the unavoidable and final break with his father. After receiving the instruction to rebuild the church, Francis hurried home to his father's place of business and gathered together some of the most valuable fabrics there in order to sell them: no money, no renovation. To be on the safe side, he rode first to the southern neighboring town, Foligno, where he sold the cloth, together with his horse, and returned to San Damiano with a handsome sum. There he offered the money for the renovation of the church to the priest, who was understandably suspicious at this turn of events. We can assume that he knew the leader of the nightly merrymakers and instinctively mistrusted this sudden conversion. He thought this strange character was trying to make a fool of him, but Francis must have remained steadfast. When he was convinced of something, he did not let up. In any case he succeeded in persuading the priest to let him live there from then on. But the priest, who apparently knew and feared the elder Bernardone, threw the money in a window niche and regarded it with contempt.

It was not primarily the loss of the money that cut Francis' father so painfully. Agitated and distraught he wandered around the town. Like a frantic investigator he scoured the area questioning all of his acquaintances to find out what had happened to his son. What he heard left him in total confusion. This was something the respected businessman could not grasp. The proud father, who had already happily anticipated his successor in the cloth business, was unable to make any sense of it. The mighty Pietro de Bernardone felt helpless and began to panic. He called his friends and neighbors together and they hurried down to San Damiano.

But the newborn knight of Christ was still a little wet behind the ears. When he saw the contingent approaching, he took to the high road and hid in one of the many caves at the foot of Mount Subasio, the principal mountain of Assisi. He still did not have the strength and the clarity to confront his father, but hid in the cave for a month, while a confidant from his parental house secretly provided him with food and drink. There, he was truly knighted and initiated, not with pomp and glory, not in the public spotlight, but in the darkness of this cave, in the belly of the whale, on the dark and still uncertain threshold of his new life.

Francis was still unsure, he still doubted his own courage, and did not yet trust his strength and staying power. The question of whether or not he could hold out, his one true wish, tortured him. Francis suffered throughout these days in his cave. He despaired and prayed, fasted and cried. It was an important but, nevertheless, painful process of purification, full of uncertainties. He was not sure how much of his sudden transformation was only a crazy idea, false vanity or a sudden burst of inspiration. He was not sure whether or not it was merely the boredom of a well-to-do son of the bourgeois, or a momentary case of religious euphoria. The knight was missing the final feeling of certainty that he was acting upon a directive of his Lord. This decisive moment, however, did not simply come from heaven in one fell swoop. It came about through the dark days he endured, when he questioned all his doubts and lived out all his fears.

Francis: What I went through in this darkness is hard to describe. Many things that happened in these years were critical for my future life. As unspectacular and lacking in honor as these weeks were on the outside, so essential they were in reality. It was an inner trembling, a spasm, a crying and shaking that I can't put into words. In this cave I went through hell. There was so much in me clamoring to be heard, it pressed down on me, fighting and gnawing inside me. Sometimes it was a storm of images: successful merchant, career man, tender lover, family man, manager of a society of dreamers, star of the poor, anti-hero. And yet as these nights wore on, the pictures slowly faded. The strange feeling of emptiness, which replaced them, became ever stronger. At first I had been moved by the triumphant dreams of Spoleto, but now those dreams, too, lost their power. All feelings of victory faded away. It was cool, damp and hard in the cave, and on some days I fasted consciously. I first believed that this was the way I could force something to happen, like becoming a hero, or something to that effect. But these self-fabricated ideas did not hold water anymore. This became more painfully evident as each day passed. I was praying now more out of desperation than piety. And I had time on my hands, a terrible lot of time, in which I became more and more afraid.

During this time I learned to fear God, as it says in the Bible. It became clear to me that this doesn't mean being afraid of God—at most I was afraid of what was going on inside me. Fear of God has much more to do with reverence and respect before the even Greater. Fear of God also involves the realization of my inability to assess things in their entirety, recognizing that I'm not all-powerful and can never have everything completely under control, that it's a waste of life to want to take charge of everything, that maybe I'm not as important as I think, that life doesn't revolve around me and that I'm a part of something much bigger than myself.

In these days it became clear to me that fear of God means becoming silent before him, listening to him, praying to him and in this way finding peace. It taught me to distinguish between the important and the unimportant, and made an even greater clarity possible. Prayers suddenly became worthwhile, if you'll excuse me for saying so. It was suddenly clear inside me that I wanted to let myself be loved by an even greater Father, who wanted the best for me. I wanted to put myself in the hands of my even greater Father, and he had plans for me. From then on it was as if he was at work inside me.

Men have a hard time trusting in something that exceeds their own strength. In this way they destroy themselves because they believe that everything depends on them alone. But how should I explain the other way to you? Maybe it's like in football or baseball: you play and you try. No champion or saint ever fell from heaven. You can see that in my example. It's the doing that counts. Endless discussions don't lead to anything. Eventually you're just going to have to take the first step.

But getting back to my cave, the training part can't always be fun. For us men there's a form of initiation that can and is allowed to hurt. Speaking from my own experience, maybe you are puffed up with pride and completely sold on yourself and you despair because the world doesn't run according to your will. This is the point. You have to learn humility, because things simply don't depend on you. Something greater is at work, and you'll only be able to accomplish something great when you become an instrument. If I can just bring up my image again, the knight first becomes great when he fights for something that is greater than himself. Every true knight acts on a directive that doesn't only come from himself alone. Otherwise he just slaves away, achieving nothing.

How do you get to this place? There is nothing very heroic about this process, which is actually more likely to cause you pain. You have to retreat—as I did in the cave—and face yourself, your goals and visions, your mistakes and guilt, your inapproachability and your limitations. This can be, depending on your situation in life, a painful and sometimes depressing phase, and it can also take time. But when you have placed yourself at the mercy of these things you will discover a new lightness of spirit and see that you have a new directive, one that is magnificent and comes from a greater source. It will be your directive, there where you are standing, where you are living and where you are needed. But not just you alone will decide.

No Longer Father Pietro di Bernardone

One day, filled with indescribable joy and a wonderful clarity, Francis stepped out of the cave, as his followers later report, and back into life. Now he was ready for whatever lay ahead. He was purified and armed for what was waiting in store for him. Inflamed with passion, as his followers describe, he set out, undaunted, on the way to Assisi. Now he was also prepared and capable of facing his father.

Thin as a rail and near to physical exhaustion, the knight of Christ entered his hometown. Not everyone would have recognized him right away, and those who did were mortified by what they saw. They made serious accusations against him, declaring him to be completely crazy or out of his mind and pelted him with dirt and stones. But where was one to go who is no longer willing to play the game? The sight of him alone must have affected them deeply. The only one who remained untouched was Francis himself.

But the critical encounter was still to come, and it did not take long before the news reached his father. Rumors about this story spread like a wild fire through the streets and alleys of Assisi. It was not as if Pietro di Bernardone had just been waiting around all this time for his son to reappear. When he learned what his fellow citizens had done to his son, he was furious. The public humiliation Francis was submitted to brought his rage to the boiling point: a mixture of anger and despair, disappointment and deep shame. The father lost every measure of self-control and something snapped inside him. Like an angry wolf he looked into his son's haggard eyes. Without a word he grabbed him, dragged him into his house and locked him in a dark chamber. There he worked on him, and not only with words. But in the meantime Francis was used to dark places.

Pietro did not want to lose his son but to bring him back into his world by any means possible. Locking him up was not such an unusual measure, as the town charter of Assisi provided this option for unusually frivolous sons, and after all, there was the stolen cloth this particular son had sold off in Foligno to get money. But for a long time now, money had not been the only concern. Still, the theft was the only thing the father could hold up to the law. It was the only concrete thing he really had. The hurt pride, the shattered hopes and deep shame counted for nothing here.

Although the mother did not necessarily approve of her husband's actions, she also tried to dissuade her son from his plan. It did no good. On the contrary, the son apparently succeeded in softening up his mother while his father was away on a business trip, so that she let him out and Francis returned to San Damiano.

After his father's return the situation finally reached a climax. At the beginning of that year, when Francis was just twenty-five years old, Pietro di Bernardone took the only legal action that was left to him and reported his son to the city council on the charge of theft. The council sent a messenger down to San Damiano, who delivered the summons to Francis. Francis, however, made it known that he was no longer under the jurisdiction of the city court, but servant of the highest God alone. This defiant and self-confident answer was, in fact, not entirely unwelcome for the council, who were consequently able to hand over the case to the bishop of Assisi and thus rid themselves of the troublesome Bernardone family matter.

Bishop Guido's summons for Francis followed, which led to the famous scene before the bishop's palace. The bishop, who had known Francis for a long time and observed his development, not without benevolence, was well informed. The up-and-coming merchant class had long been a thorn in the church's side and, also, Bishop Guido saw the threat of sinfulness in the accumulation of money and trade. Thus for him the fronts were clearly drawn from the beginning, and in his eyes Pietro di Bernardone was only after the money.

He told Francis to give the money back to his father and then his anger would undoubtedly be soothed. Besides, because it was most likely money gained by sinful means, it would also not be good to use it for construction of the church.

Francis knew that things would not be resolved this easily, just as he knew at that moment that more than money was involved, that in fact everything was at stake. Strengthened by the bishop's support, which was indeed the first official recognition he had received since daring to leave the cave, he finally confronted his father and his past.

He did not want to return only the money but also the clothes and everything else he had gotten from his father. Francis disappeared into one of the bishop's chambers, removed his clothes and laid the money on top of them. Before the eyes of the bishop, his father and all of those standing around—we can assume that in the meantime the scene had drawn a large and interested crowd of onlookers—Francis stepped out of the palace naked and said: *Up to now I have called Pietro di Bernardone my father. Because I have decided to serve God I want to return to him the money and the clothes I have received from him. From now on I will say, Our Father who art in heaven and no longer father Pietro di Bernardone.*

That hit home. Filled with pain and anger, the father took the money and the clothing—and here the father was just like his son—without leaving Francis with so much as a pair of underwear, which outraged many of the onlookers. He did not have anything left here to do, or better said, had lost everything. He grimly trudged away in silence, his son's belongings under his arm. A few cries of protest still reached him, but left him unmoved. There was nothing more to do. The father had understood the message clearly. A few of the onlookers were so shaken they began to cry. They felt sorry for the young man, but they did not see the knight, who was already far beyond their sympathy. Bishop Guido, who realized what was going on with this man of God, took Francis in his arms and covered him with his cloak.

Now all the bridges had been burned. Francis finally left the world behind him, as he once later formulated. He left behind the world of the material, the world of his father and the world of the middle class, with all its security, the world of his previous life. In doing so he did not have a clear vision of how things should continue, but only knew his directive to rebuild the little church in San Damiano. And that was also where he returned.

> **Francis**: *Yes, the scene before the bishop's palace was not without consequences—my fate was sealed. At that time I didn't think for very long about what I should do next or how I should do it. One step just followed the next. Neither of us had a choice any longer. And this was exactly the way it had to be. We both knew this as we stood facing each other. But I can understand that it still hurt him.*
>
> *There was no more hate inside me, no arrogance, but only clarity. Another greater Father had adopted me.*

In this respect I wasn't fatherless, but I couldn't bring the two fathers together anymore and I knew clearly where I belonged. And I only gave him back his possessions; anything else would have been presumptuous. I know that I had gotten more from him than his money and clothing.

I gave him back the material world I wanted to break free of. In this regard it was a letting go. But you can only give back what you have received. The path I took probably would have not been possible had my father not taken his own path. Many men today bleed from the wounds received from their father, and when they speak of manliness their eyes are sad. Maybe it would help if we started to think about our fathers in a more forgiving way. There are basically three ways to solve a problem. You can change it, leave it behind you or love it. And it is no different with our father problems.

Change: This doesn't mean that you should change your father, but rather your relationship. Many sons would like nothing better than to change their fathers, but this is something that we are not entitled to do. Your father existed before you and you have him to thank for your life, irrespective of what he was like. Without him you wouldn't be here. It is your right to make things better or different, but it is presumptuous to want to change your father as a person. My father's story always remains a different one than mine and my story isn't his. You can try to change your relationship. Some sons complain continually about their fathers, instead of telling them what they would like from them, what they need from them. But to do this they first have to get down off their high horses because nothing can get better with moralistic reproaches. If this way isn't possible, then there are two other possibilities.

Leaving: This was no doubt my way. And it might be that solution of the problem isn't possible without separation. Then it's all right to simply go another way. So that this separation is really a solution, you also have to separate yourselves inwardly and with dignity. Say that's your life and this is mine. As long as you need your father as a scapegoat, as an excuse, as a bad example, you won't be free of him. You carry the problem constantly inside you. Breaking free also means letting go, leaving him alone, leaving him in peace. Otherwise this way won't help. When I gave back the clothes to my father, I was inwardly almost reconciled with him. I never said to anyone, don't become like my father. The surest way to become like one's own father is by making a desperate attempt to try to become anything else in the world but him.

Love: First, this way accepts and honors the father for the person he is. To do this does not mean retreating to the role of the little boy who idolizes his father and puts him on a pedestal, which is no longer possible and would only be self-deception. This solution, though, can be especially problematic when wounds and hurt were inflicted. I would like to show you a way that can create reconciliation.

Imagine yourself in your father's past life and in his life with his father. Did he receive himself what you expect of him? Did he have a father who could give him what he would then be able to pass on? Did someone show him through example the way he should treat his own children?

The serious attempt to understand another person can be the first step toward loving him. This also applies, by the way, when your father is no longer living. Sometimes it can also be important to clarify something at a later time, perhaps even at the cemetery. And one more thing: it does us good to simply pray: Our Father who art in heaven—something I would just like to add from my own experience. This all sounds pretty dramatic, and for a lot of men it is. There are also many men who have had good relationships with their fathers who could learn from them and enjoy talking about them. They sense that this has to do with their own masculinity, something that cannot be passed on from the mother to her son. Only a man can finally convey to a son what it means to be a man. This is also why the father theme is important for men. My leavetaking at that time was that of a man. I did not run to my mother but went to other men, and ultimately a community was created that I never could have imagined at that time in my life.

But you could also see my scene before the bishop's palace in a much simpler way. Scripture tells us that we have to leave our father and mother. This does not only count for members of orders like me, but for each of you when you marry. Then, also, you have to leave your father and mother so that you can begin something new with your wife. It must be a new way and take its own form. To do this it is necessary to abandon the familiar ties and safe havens, which you and your wife then build up together anew. I don't know much about women and marriage, but the situations are probably not so dissimilar. So that something new may come into being the old has to be left behind. It's not possible to have everything and courage belongs to life. I also didn't know at that time how things would ultimately continue. But I did what was necessary and honest.

GOING INSTEAD OF WAITING

Francis stood naked in front of the city gates, and it was a cold time of the year. Not only did his body need protection but also his very existence needed protecting. And what exactly was he now anyway? He was naked in every respect. At that time there were more than enough religious zealots and sectarians whose existence was not without danger. Was he now a man without rights, an outlaw or an oddball whom everyone could treat as he or she saw fit? He also needed a social cloak. At that time the church recognized the status of penitents, and Francis found a hermit's habit and donned it. With a staff in his hand, sandals on his feet and a leather strap as a belt, he returned to San Damiano. He had run away for the last time. The priest there would have noticed that something was amiss with the young man, and would have provided him with food, if only because the church was responsible for such penitents. But the priest presumably did not feel completely at ease with the situation.

The directive of the crucifix in San Damiano had not changed, and water still dripped from the ceiling of the little church. Things were serious now and Francis got started with the work of rebuilding the chapel. He was not a trained brick-layer, and the little church was no architectural masterpiece. Presumably both Francis and the priest would have thought that somehow things would work out. In any case hard work was involved and the spoiled young man from Assisi had to carry it out. He slaved and toiled away, sometimes completely without a plan. The first night he slept the sleep of the exhausted. The priest was taken with his eagerness, astonished at his commitment and, although he was poor himself, made sure that the young man had at least an extra ration of food. After all, he knew how extravagantly Francis had lived up to now. At some point the stones ran out and even all Francis' prayers could not change that. He set off for his hometown. He was not sure exactly what would happen next, but it made no difference. At the same time there were many who—rightfully or wrongfully—thought him a fool when he entered town and began, almost if he were drunk, singing songs of praise to the Lord. At some point he came to his senses and invented the "lottery of stones for heaven," meaning, if someone gave him two stones the donor's rewards would be twofold and if someone gave him three stones the rewards would be threefold and so on. In such matters Francis was unlearned and naive. He was not an educated theologian, trained preacher or expert in nonprofit fundraising. But he needed stones for the little church in San Damiano.

Francis spoke with the fire of the spirit. He was able to move people, but it was not with clever words or ingenious arguments. If there was ever an anti-intellectual who achieved more than anyone else, it was Francis. On this day there were more than a few who laughed at this strange bird, thinking he had finally gone off the deep end. But others were full of empathy, some even moved to tears. They naturally all knew his past and therefore his very different side. Now he stood in front of them in the poor garb of a penitent, singing and talking about stones. Francis was a sight who could not be matched. And it was not long before he did not have to drag the stones up to the chapel himself. People arrived daily in San Damiano with stones, and some even hoisted them into place.

Without a doubt Francis felt a sense of achievement, and the priest looked around for additional provisions to give the motivated young man. For it even says in the Bible that whoever works should also eat. The priest felt responsible for the young penitent, who was primarily occupied with fulfilling his directive and sleeping soundly every evening. In the middle of work there is little time for reflection. But as soon as sufficient stones had arrived, been put in their place, the worst patched up, the roof made watertight and the crucifix secured, the man of action found quiet time again. It was at that point that he probably first noticed his extra ration.

As much as Francis enjoyed what he was doing now, his current situation occupied his thoughts constantly, especially since his directive was nearing its end. Slowly but surely the question arose in his mind about how things should proceed afterward and what his next instructions would be. He had dreamt both his dreams, experienced the embrace of the leper as well as his directive before the crucifix, the weeks in the cave and the encounter with his father, and now the chapel was almost finished. But how should things go on, the hermit asked himself: was this alone his way?

> **Francis:** *I have to speak up here, because it is just this point of uncertainty that is important. At that moment I had no idea how things would proceed. Everyone is taught to first look, then decide and then take action. That sounds totally reasonable, and theoretically speaking it's right. In my case it wasn't this way, as you probably have already noticed. But what's it like with you? It's not seldom that you first look and then the endless discussion begins. This is considered sensible and clever, though the final product is more often than not long-winded palaver. It's especially the most educated*

who often don't do anything at all, believing that clever-
ness alone is enough.

Sometimes you men speak for hours about a multi-
tude of clever things, and what you say isn't wrong
either. But there aren't any consequences. You don't do or
change anything, and then everything else is worthless.
Talking is free of charge and therefore you can talk for-
ever and nothing happens. If the only purpose of your
talking is to blow your own horn then you can just forget
it. It's worthless and doesn't change anything. It is just
another form of self-gratification, flight and anxiety. This
could also be adapted from Scriptures: You will know
them by their speech.

At this point in time, many things had finally been
decided for good and many things were still open for me.
After all of the events up to this time, I really had no idea
how things would go on. But I did something. You might
think it was dumb and reckless, but something grew out
of it, step by step. In comparison, all the endless discus-
sion is in the true sense of the word impotent. This much
I learned: it doesn't change anything. How many of you
men talk so cleverly, but then when it finally comes down
to taking action it's a washout. Then the same old tired
excuses resound: I didn't mean it that way. That's not the
right way to understand it. That's not the way it's sup-
posed to be. You can't expect something like that.

Life is a risk and it will always be. But we can't just
stop and wait. We have to do something. We have to form
our life, make decisions, set values, follow them and take
action. You can't envision how your life is going to turn
out before you take a step forward. That's not the way the

threads of life are woven. At the end of his days such a man went before God, who then asked him what he had done in his life. The man answered, "The whole time I thought about what I should do." God replied, "I think I'll do the same thing now with you. Only I have all eternity to do it."

You have so much fear. That's why you remain so long looking and judging. That's something you can really do for an eternity. You first often try to determine if it's right before you take action. I know this sounds crazy, but only when you first set out are you in a position to gauge your way, to determine rightness or wrongness. You are welcome to make mistakes and get stuck in dead ends. All of this is better than not setting off at all, because you'll find your way out of the dead ends again, and we've only ourselves to blame if we make the same mistake more than twice. Life is a challenge and it remains that way. To finish at the starting line is the greatest waste of all.

THE FATHERLY BLESSING

It was like a blank space that was almost filled up, with the next one to come not yet visible. Francis could not stop thinking about the extra ration the priest slipped him. If this were his path, then he would have to have a priest beside him his whole life supplying him with food. Francis remembered the leper. Actually, what he really wanted was to share the life of the poor, and now although he did slave away and was thoroughly beat and tired every evening, he was still provided with food by a well-meaning priest and even given an additional ration. This could not be all there was. Despite the determination to follow his path, Francis stood time and again before choices, before crossroads, which were not yet marked. But he kept on going.

It was poverty that had led him to the reconstruction of San Damiano. The extra ration stood in sharp contrast to the leper he had embraced. The knight of Christ reminded himself of his bride, Lady Poverty. As much as he toiled inside the walls of San Damiano, this was not the life of the poor he had chosen. So how did the poor live?

The answer was his directive: Go from door to door with a bowl in your hand and put the scraps you are given into it. The embrace of the leper was the start. What now followed was no less terrible and cost no less will power for Francis. He made up his mind to beg and journeyed up to Assisi with a bowl in his hand. This had nothing to do with his earlier attempt at begging in Rome, as now he had made up his mind to eat what was given to him. Now it was serious. Francis trudged up to town and entered the city gates, filled with what must have been some hesitation and much strength of inner will. More was involved than the unappetizing question of what he would eat this evening. The bourgeois son of a merchant entered his hometown for the first time as a beggar.

Francis wanted to live a life of poverty by choice, out of love to the one who was born poor, who lived poor and who died naked on the cross. This was, however, not a slogan in a high school yearbook or a romantic social inspiration following a moving Sunday homily. What Francis planned to do he put into action in a moment and what he said he meant literally. So he stood there with his twenty-five years, in a gray hermit's habit in the streets of Assisi and proceeded, with a bowl in his hand, to beg door to door for something to eat. The people who knew how pampered a life he had led previously were astonished when they saw him take various scraps in the same bowl with such little regard for himself.

But the second part of the exercise was still to come. When he wanted to eat the mishmash of food, he was repulsed and his throat tightened up. In the past he had not even been able to look at something like that. Francis began to eat, slowly and with great self-control. Then what had occurred before happened again. It was again like the time he had embraced the leper. Not one bite stuck in his throat, he no longer gagged—it worked. A thankful happiness overcame him, and it now seemed as if he had a bowl full of delicacies before him. A transformation took place again. And what had been bitter now became sweet.

During these days his father entered the plan for the last time. His beloved son standing in the street like this, gaunt and emaciated, freezing from the cold, the gray rags hanging from his thin shoulders, in his hand a bowl with the whole town's weekly menu . . . he could not take it anymore. Shame and sympathy filled him with pain. He was not even able to avoid him now, for he was continually turning up around every corner. Pietro di Bernardone could no longer stand to see Francis. And one day the father cursed his son.

Many who had at first laughed at the beggar now stopped in their tracks and became silent; they were more than a little shocked when they saw how patiently he took it. But then Francis adopted a new father. He called to a simple man among the bystanders and said, *When you see how my father curses me, I say to you, bless me, father! And you will bless me in his place.* After the man had blessed him as he wished, Francis said to Pietro di Bernardone, *Don't you believe that God can give me a father who blesses me against your curse?*

> ***Francis****: This event was very important for me. It would have been better if my father and I had not seen each other again for a long time. My appearance was a continual provocation for him. I can understand well that he could no longer stand the sight of me. It hurt him in his innermost father's soul. When people from town ridiculed or laughed at me, it was easy for me to disregard it. But when my father cursed me it stopped being easy. That cut me deeply. It was the hardest scene between us because it was truly a curse and I needed a blessing.*
>
> *On this day it was no longer enough to say, Our Father, who art in heaven. I felt naked inside, lonely and almost lost. The last time it was a leave-taking with strength, but this time I felt helpless. It was as if I inwardly fell to my knees. My eyes fell upon an older man in the crowd who looked at me with astonishment, but*

also with kindness in his eyes. Then I knew what I needed—not reassurance, but a blessing. And I needed his blessing.

I was convinced that I was on the right path. It was not desperation that tortured me at this moment. All of a sudden I felt no strength inside me. It was as if there wasn't anyone standing behind me anymore. It was a spontaneous inspiration that led me to take this substitute father and get his blessing. And suddenly it was there again. I stood up straight once more, again full of vitality and the knowledge of what needed to be done. It was almost arrogant how I said this to my father's face. One moment I was on the ground and the next I was bursting with power.

Take this fatherly blessing for yourselves sometime. If you don't want to ask your own father for it, then look for another older man. Sometimes we don't only need advice but a blessing. Maybe something's been on your mind for a long time and inwardly you've already made a decision. You know it's the right thing to do, so this isn't what's bothering you. It just seems that something's missing. Your decision doesn't have strength yet, and you're still hesitating for one reason or another. Go to your fatherly man and tell him what you're planning. If he then says, Do it!, then you are able to sense what you still needed. This can be the missing part that bestows a blessing on your plan. What you are planning becomes a directive and the blessing gives you extra power.

WITHOUT FEAR OF FLYING

At this time Francis not only renovated San Damiano but also the church of San Pietro della Spina, which no longer exists today, and the chapel of the Portiuncula. He had forbidden the priest to give him any more extra rations. He could support himself and get the materials he needed for the renovation of the churches by doing whatever occasional work he could find and by begging. Somehow his persistent manner, which refused to abandon the pursuit of his objectives, was infectious. Again and again he found residents of the town who supported him at his construction sites. He returned to the places where he had celebrated festivals with them and begged for oil from the troubadours in French, so the lights in San Damiano could burn continually.

This passage of life, which as yet did not have a clear goal at its end, had already taken four years. Francis was not just an instant saint who came out of a can of godly revelations. His transformation was much more a long, sometimes bright, sometimes dark path, a process that led him through many stations where he knew highs and lows, sometimes secure in the knowledge of what to do and sometimes following his course without a clue. Francis set off when he did not yet know how his journey should continue, when he did not yet have an idea what its goal would be. But he set off. He followed an inner calling that was only a voice in the fog at first, but he let himself be called. He attempted and experimented, including the ridiculous scene where he masqueraded as a beggar in front of the Church of St. Peter. He still had a long way to go when he was just beginning to take on responsibility for himself, for his dream and soon for his first fellow brother.

Maybe it was more feelings of uncertainty that led him to renovate the other two chapels. It must have already been clear to him that he would not go down in history as an untrained restorer of chapels. At that time he could scarcely even have imagined his very different contribution to the restoration of the church. Francis was a man who thought in concrete terms and the instructions he had previously received before the crucifix in San Damiano comprised a concrete directive. At some point, when he was climbing around on the stonework he surely would have asked himself if this was all, and what was going to come next—but only sometimes, for he had a lot to do.

Francis was a bundle of energy and possessed a deep inner strength, but it was still unclear what form his life would take. So much inside him was in movement. He knew the essentials, but a concrete model was still missing. There were his dreams and the image of the Crucified One, there was the restorer, the beggar and the knight of poverty, but there was no rhyme or reason to it. The frame was missing to complete the picture. The thread running through these years, from one chapel to the next, from one task to another, leading ahead to the future, was missing. Again this time it was hardly an accident when at the beginning of 1208, at the age of twenty-six, he went again to San Damiano and heard the Gospel during Mass. Francis now needed something concrete.

Jesus' sending out of his disciples was a concrete gospel if there ever was one: *The kingdom of heaven is at hand . . . do not take gold or silver or copper in your belts. Do not take a sack for your journey, or a second tunic or sandals, or walking stick. For whoever works deserves his keep. . . . When you enter*

*a house say first, Peace be with this house! If you are invited
inside the house, stay there and eat and drink what you are
offered.* Was it really this easy? Or had he missed something?
After Mass Francis went to the priest and questioned him. Is that
really written there and is it supposed to be understood that
way? Yes, it's really written there, and that was how it was to be
understood. Francis was a practical man. He did not need philo-
sophical interpretations but clear guidance for a solid directive.
This quote was as clear and concrete as he needed. It seemed
that they had both been waiting for each other. This was exactly what he wanted! An indescribable happiness filled him when
he said this aloud. The priest read the Gospel to him again and
in a short time he knew the passage by heart. He kept it in his
memory the rest of his life.

Now he had what he had been searching for so long: a clear
directive that extended beyond the next construction site. On
this day and in this Gospel his long years of striving and searching found their final model—and a definitive one at that. It was
no less than Christ's directive to his disciples that gave Francis
his own directive for life. In the sending-out of the disciples he
recognized his calling. The giver of instructions was in both
cases the same. This is something Francis attached great importance to his entire life. His directive did not come from the
church, from a priest or anyone else. His directive, and he
repeated this in his *Testament,* came from the Lord. Even if
Francis was not a church rebel, he changed much just by the
way he lived and thus the great importance he attached to this
point becomes understandable. Despite all of his loyalty to the
church there was never any question in his mind that he had
received his instructions directly from God.

These were considerable footsteps he was walking in, and he

was never one to lack self-confidence. He followed in the apostles' footsteps so that we would remember them. He followed in these footsteps to remind us that Christ does not provide his disciples with only comfortable house slippers, and that Christian faith loses its strength when it is watered down to become a trimming of middle-class prosperity, when it was always thought of as something much more radical. Just to make it perfectly clear: certainly no person was more able to do this than Francis. He did not beat around the bush but immediately put his directive into action. In his mind, interpretation or analysis was useless.

Without hesitating he cast off everything—he got rid of his shoes, staff and sack, and exchanged the hermit's habit for a rough, unsightly robe. So as not even to be tempted to take anything with him, he threw away the belt and fastened his robe with a rope instead. He avoided every possession from that time on and scorned coins like the plague. More than once he ground them into the dirt with his foot, saying that was the only way to deal with such a temptation from the devil. Now he was finally free.

> ***Francis:*** *I also felt free, free as a bird that could fly because a burden had been lifted from him—free and light. Now you'll probably think I'm completely crazy, but that's the way it was and that's the way it is. That's how it is with the birds of the sky and the lilies of the field. It was an incredible feeling, and yet at the same time I felt like I was standing on absolutely solid ground. It was reality.*
>
> *That's easy for him to say, I hear you saying. And you aren't completely wrong. Up to that point I hadn't had any responsibility for other people. But just the same, if you can't fly it also has to do with you. You cling to so*

much of what makes you unfree and isn't even necessary. How many of you aren't satisfied with what fulfills
your needs? It always has to be more and more, always
better, faster, more fantastic, and what the other person
has, you need, too, but even bigger. Just try to figure out
the time that a lot of men spend slaving for status symbols. Your worries grow bigger with the more you pile up,
and what's supposed to make your life easier actually
only makes it more complicated. At the same time you
become tired inside, old, feeble and too weary to fly. Life
has passed you by and you didn't even notice it.

I never expected that all people should live like me.
Later I even forbade my brothers to speak badly of those
who didn't live like we did. Even more the questions are
whether or not you can still feel life, whether or not you are
happy, and whether, at least sometimes, you can still fly.

THE NIGHT WITH THE BROTHER

Now the second part of the directive followed and concerned the form his life would take. In his new outfit and filled with an indescribable strength, he went up to the city again and began to preach. He called himself simple and uneducated, *idiota* in the Latin of his day, and stood in the market square of Assisi preaching repentance. Theologically speaking what he preached would not have been especially original, made up of Bible passages he could memorize easily. But people stopped and listened in astonishment. Here was someone who practiced what he preached, a person who looked first at himself instead of always starting with others. It was much less the words that really hit home than his whole person. Francis himself was the sermon that won them over. When the little barefoot man with the mild yet fiery eyes preached about peace, it wasn't seldom that longtime squabblers suddenly fell into each other's arms.

For the people of Assisi, it became more and more difficult *not* to take this strange young man seriously, because the effect he had on people was ultimately an uncomfortable one and one that was not easy to ignore. As soon as someone took him seriously there were unavoidable consequences. One could not simply go back and pretend that everything was the same as before. For those in whom he struck an even deeper chord there was no turning back. The first of these was Bernard of Quintavalle.

They knew each other from the past and Bernard had long observed the change in Francis, as he now enthusiastically slaved away repairing the dilapidated churches, whereas in his former pampered existence he had always lived just for the day.

Bernard saw Francis preaching in his coarse robe, fastened
around his middle with a rope, even while continuing to remain
in the background himself. And Francis did not look the least bit
unhappy. Bernard had always imagined penitents to look as if
they were suffering. This one, however, was in high spirits, his
whole face radiant. He looked more transfigured than languish-
ing. And what he said was simply the truth; there was no way
around it. The penny had already dropped when Bernard secretly approached Francis one day on a side street and asked if he
could talk to him. Dusk had fallen when Francis entered his
house. There the two men sat across from each other and stayed
up talking the whole night. Both were excited in happy expectation of what was to come, yet in fact everything was already
clear. Something was in the air and it just had to be put into
words. Some marriages must also have been arranged in a mood
like this. For the two men much changed on this night, in fact,
their whole lives. What was a person to do with his possessions
when he didn't want them anymore? Bernard asked. It was a
rhetorical question. Some time in the course of the evening his
declaration came: I want to give everything to the poor and follow your way of life. Now it was out, and for Bernard there was
no return ticket either. Francis knew that this man was serious.
A feeling of jubilation overcame him, for until now he had been
alone and now he had a companion. Some time in this night the
thought presumably would have come that he himself was also
standing at a crossroad. It is wonderful not to be alone anymore,
but it changes life in a radical way. Every hour that can be
shared with another is shortened, and trust and support are
shared, as well as help and a common basis. On the other hand,
order would be necessary, and also mutual agreement and con-
sideration. On this night when a loner became two brothers, the

first euphoria was mixed with uncertainty in the dawn of the
new day.

> *Francis: I'll never forget that night. We sat across from
> each other, excited and restless, both of us filled with
> anticipation. Our hearts were full and our mouths over-
> flowed with words. But what were these words? Who
> should begin? Two men in love with the same idea sat
> across from each other. And it was really as if we were
> waiting for one of us to make the first move. As men fac-
> ing men we didn't have any experience with such things.
> Maybe that's why we were so uncertain. There are such
> strange fears that overcome two men when they want to
> show their feelings.*
>
> *I can't really say anymore which one of us was the
> first to open up. At first it was a cautious announcement,
> a peculiar sounding out of each other, although we both
> knew what was going on and both saw it in each other's
> eyes. Men can certainly act strangely around each other
> when it comes down to what really counts. As happy as I
> was that this respectable guy wanted to join me on my
> path of life, I was uncertain at the same time. We men can
> behave peculiarly with each other. In this night of engage-
> ment—and you can go ahead and call it that—there was
> the happiness about not being alone anymore, but also
> the uncertainty of what was to come. I, also not one to
> jump up and give free reign to my feelings, was some-
> what hesitant as I asked myself how my life would
> change. Up to now I hadn't had to take anyone else into
> account. I could pray, eat, preach, sleep, beg and dream
> when and how I darn well pleased—excuse me for saying*

that, but that's the way it was. I was happy about a shared life, but it became more and more clear that a lot of things would change, even down to the insignificant matters of daily life. This night wasn't only about the feelings of us two men but also about a decision. I suspect that with you and your women it's not any different. But it was good so. That night was unforgettable.

As Fools in the World

Peter di Cantanio seemed to have been waiting for this moment, because he also wanted to join Francis, and it was as if he had been nearby, looking for his chance the whole night. Peter, from a family of respected nobility, wealthy and highly educated, was likewise deeply touched, affected in such a way that there was no going back. In any case on the way to the church in the market square they had already become a group of three. Francis was enthralled and at the same time uncertain, for now he was to bear responsibility for two fellow brothers. For him alone everything was clear, but on this night the situation had changed. He searched once more for proof, in the form of the book oracle, which he knew from the popular pious tradition. In church he opened the Scriptures three times and three times he found passages about Jesus sending out his disciples and the radical form of this discipleship. Whether or not Bernard or Peter, who both knew Latin, helped out remains an open question. In addition to the Gospel he had heard in San Damiano, Francis found similar passages. This was the confirmation he had searched for, what he needed for himself and his two companions, as if he said, "Brothers, this is the life and the rule for us and everyone who wants to join us!"

A few days later the small community received another follower. Egidius, the fourth in the group, was a laborer who did not have as much to give away as the other two but possessed a robust nature and was eager to roll up his sleeves and join in. They lived as itinerate preachers in the area around Assisi, carrying out occasional jobs for which they accepted only what they needed to live. If there was not enough for all four they begged for alms. A lean-to made of boards near the Portiuncula served as more of a common meeting place than a real place to stay. They lived the life of the poor openly and in a radical way, even when they were increasingly met with resistance. This was one of the reasons they separated one day to go through the country preaching. The merchant and the laborer, Francis and Egidius, wandered in the province of Marken while Bernard and Peter stayed in Umbria. Their meeting place remained the shack by the Portiuncula.

In spite of any animosity from outside, the four men were happy, and it was more than the kick of an alternative lifestyle—for this their life was too hard and rough. It was more than putting on a happy face in the midst of a grueling existence. They were free of earthly demands and limitations. The happiness they radiated was the expression of their inner freedom, the freedom of the dislocated, and when Francis was especially happy he lifted his voice and sang French songs, which Egidius could probably only hum along to. They were the troubadours of the Lord, Francis said, and this was probably where their special fascination lay as they called the public to repent and atone. The Lord's wandering minstrels lived the Gospels through their own example. As court jesters of their society who were able to be truthful, they placed themselves in opposition to the world and its pursuits, held a mirror in front of their contemporaries of what was essential, in which the most dogged pursuits were turned on their head. Probably the biggest cause of provocation was that these fools in the world, as Francis once called himself, had the most to laugh about and were the most cheerful of all. As a community of brothers they were raised up by their ideals and dedicated themselves to serving them. Their life as brothers bonded them even further. Together they were even stronger.

Francis: This was an important part of my life, and one of the best parts. It does men good to be together in a truly brotherly sense. Men experience each other most of the time as rivals and as if they are at battle, whether openly or secretly, wrangling for recognition and position, for a place in the pecking order. Often it is a secret fight for territory, even more so when a woman is involved. At the local hangout there is a kind of truce— or not—and even then, just to be on the safe side, they talk only about trivial matters. Sometimes one of the guys even pats himself on the back to show how great he is, but there's hardly any talk about what's important, or what touches an individual personally. Who can easily say in their regular hangout, "Hey, everybody, I have a problem"?

But, excuse me, men don't have problems. How hypocritical this male culture is. Everyone feels the same feelings and each person has a burden to bear, but heaven forbid he should talk about it. The knight doesn't open his visor in front of other knights for fear he might get hit. But you throw away a lot of chances that way.

It does so much good when the stags vying for territory are able to check their antlers at the door. I don't claim that we never had any problems like that. In the end we were just men, too. But I wish for you what we experienced. It didn't matter what or who someone was. We were neither hiding in a suit of armor nor did we have to prove anything to each other. We were brothers among brothers and that's an incredible feeling. It wasn't an attitude of sentimental weepiness, but a source of self-assured manliness. We lost the fear of each other and could suddenly behave with care and attention, even with tenderness, toward one another, yet the path we took was one of men. This doesn't mean we were always giving each other bear hugs, but we sensed each other as brothers and this held an incredible power.

OTHERWISE, WE NEED WEAPONS

The society defended itself against its court jesters. The citizens of Assisi could live with just Francis, but now it seemed a contagious illness had broken out. No father could be certain that his son would not fall victim to the same craziness. People thought Francis and his brothers were mentally ill, and fearful girls and women made a detour around them. Some mocked them, threw dirt at them and even took away their robes, leaving them standing naked on a public street. Still others grabbed their hoods from behind and dragged them away on their backs. They were as free as birds, yet they did not put up any resistance, did not curse, and the most annoying thing was that everything could be taken from them by force except their cheerfulness.

When they returned to the Portiuncula from their first missionary trip, three more men joined them. The city found itself in a state of turmoil, and the uncertainty increased with the number of respected citizens who joined the community of brothers. The situation was not without danger, especially since at that time there were more than a few religious sects on the move who could easily have been confused with the brothers. One day Bishop Guido called the alleged troublemaker to him and tried to restrain him with well-meaning words, telling him this way of life was really much too hard after all, and living without any possessions just wasn't realistic. But there was nothing left for Bishop Guido to say when he heard the response Francis gave him: *If we had possessions, there would be strife and quarreling, and we would need weapons to guard them.* Poverty and peace were one component in Francis' eyes.

Francis: *I know that for you it's not possible to do completely without possessions and so I don't want to stress you. But if you're honest you know this connection. As soon as you want more than you need, then commotion starts and peace is over. This already begins with your inner peace. All at once you start piling up things and looking around covetously at what you might be missing, and you don't even know anymore what you really want. This gets you off kilter. And it's how things keep going until you really need weapons, most of them today more complex than a sword. Then one hand washes the other, and you are no longer able to escape from the downward spiral.*

Money alone doesn't bring happiness, and without money it's not possible to live. I learned at least that much. You have to find the point where possessions bring you security and add to your happiness. But beyond that the tide turns and you become restless, devoid of peace and no longer able to even enjoy what you have. Maybe I'm not an expert on enjoyment, but that's how things are, you can believe me. In case you don't, then check yourself again, look at yourself in the mirror of truth, if you are able to be this honest.

OF ENTHUSIASM AND ORDER

The Bishop of Assisi alone could not protect them during this dangerous time, especially since the little troupe was making an ever greater circle in their wanderings, often occupied outside of the area of their town. In the spring of 1209—Francis was at that time twenty-seven years old and the number of brothers had increased to twelve—they changed from being the forge to being the blacksmith. They composed a paper that was intended as the rule of their order. It was mostly made up of the Bible passages they had found at the time of the book oracle about the discipleship of Christ. The paper was not a canonical book of rules, although Peter, because of his education, would have been familiar with such a thing. It was more of a concise but authentic expression of their form of life. The shared enthusiasm should be the determining factor, and not a piece of paper. But in fact an audience before the pope was not possible without it.

Outwardly it was a pitiful bunch that arrived in Rome at that time. But beneath the gray, dirty robes, sparkling eyes shone from radiant faces, and there was something contagious about their spirit. Although one could question them with a critical eye, it was really not possible to put up a fight against them. Pope Innocent III must have felt something similar when he saw the self-assured group in front of him. It was certainly not the norm that visitors in Rome could have a papal audience whenever they pleased. Bishop Guido had pulled a few strings and a cardinal of the Curia first tried to place them in one of the existing orders. In Francis' case he was fighting a losing battle. His directive came straight from heaven. The Lord himself was giving him instructions, and if he had been a Benedictine, an Augustinian or a Cistercian then his directive would have been different. His self-confidence in the face of the highest curia was enormous, and in terms of church politics more than a little dangerous, but still everyone must have sensed it was not a product of his imagination or a personal conjecture. He lived every word he said. Something was at work within him. In any case the pope confirmed their community, if only in spoken form.

Shared enthusiasm has far-reaching effects. Nevertheless a trip from Assisi to Rome on foot is something that calls for organizational decisions to be made. Which way should we go? Where should we spend the night? Can we make it to the next village before the thunderstorm reaches us? Where and what should we eat? What about a bath in the lake? The birds of the skies and the lilies of the fields suddenly saw themselves confronted with practical things, which was not Francis' area of expertise. For him everything should have taken its own course. During the time he was alone such silly questions had never come up. Somehow they agreed that Bernard should take over this job. He was to say how and where they should proceed and the others would follow. This made everything easier. But in Rome it was again indisputably clear who the boss was.

> **Francis**: *This topic was always troublesome for me. There are men who are simply good at what wasn't the least bit important to me, but without which things don't seem to function. None of us felt like continually discussing trivial matters. But we would still have to choose our way. With you it is often considered very up to date and important to discuss such matters in great detail. But in fact in such discussions most of the time is actu-*

*ally spent talking about things that are completely incon-
sequential, and at some point the consequential things
get mixed into it and then you end up with a real mess.*

*I admit that in Rome this was also not an issue any-
more. I wouldn't have given up the leadership there, and
no one would have expected it of me. But I didn't feel like
discussing where we should spend the night. I know that
in our order obedience also took on other proportions
later, but here it had to do with pragmatic matters and I
was happy that I could turn all of this over to Bernard. I
also never meddled in how he handled things.
Presumably he just didn't get much from it himself,
because he always had to try to keep up with everyone's
thoughts while I could remain with mine alone.*

*Still I admit this task was important. Leadership is
a service to others, who are then able to let go of some of
their burdens and become free for themselves. In any
case taking care of organizational detail was never my
cup of tea. For this reason I am more grateful then ever
to Bernard for taking it on. Apparently it's easier for us
men when a certain order is present and we don't have
to talk continually about every possible kind of foolish-
ness. Maybe that sounds pretty backward to you, but just
look at your own life. We each had different roles and in
this way things functioned well.*

SIMPLE IS NOT SO SIMPLE

After their return from Rome the twelve brothers settled in Rivotorto, an idyllic area in the valley below the city of Assisi. A little creek wound its way through turnip fields, meadows and olive groves. There they found an abandoned shack, which served as their first lodgings. However, it was so cramped inside they all had hardly enough room to lie down, and Francis wrote their names on the ceiling beams so that each person had a place for himself alone. Some found occasional work on farms, others begged, while some helped out in the nearby hospital for lepers. In the evening they joined each other for a shared meal. Despite the cramped conditions and poverty it was a happy time—a "honeymoon" spent by the young brotherhood in Rivotorto following their endorsement by the pope.

These were no feasts they partook of and also included an observance of the rules of fasting. One night in the crowded hut one of the brothers cried out aloud, "I'm dying!" Francis asked him what was wrong and the brother replied he was starving to death. Francis set the table and woke up all of the brothers, instructing them to eat with this brother so he would not be ashamed. Naturally, he added later, this didn't give everyone the right to do whatever he pleased whenever he wanted, but they all had to be aware of their individual needs and everyone's needs were different. In their enthusiasm an overly zealous penitential desire had arisen and some brothers even acquired iron penitential belts, which Francis strictly forbade. No brother was allowed to wear anything on his body except his robe. Everyone must respect his body and give it what was necessary. This applied to all of them—except him and Brother Ass.

In time they became bothersome to the farmers of Rivotorto, especially since the group was growing in number all the time. One day a farmer drove his donkey backwards into the shack with the announcement that he wanted to pay them his respects, choosing this means of expression to do so. Francis got the hint and started looking for a new place to live. He had wanted an official place to settle his new order anyway, where there should also be a chapel for the prayer of the Liturgy of the Hours and celebration of Mass. At that time individual priests were already among them. He went to Bishop Guido and the canon with this request but got only negative responses. After that he asked the abbot of the Benedictine cloister at the foot of Mount Subasio and received the Portiuncula, the poorest chapel in the area, which he had halfway gotten into shape some time ago. Francis was poor but still thought like a merchant. As he loathed every possession, he agreed with the bishop to a leasing fee of one basket of fish per year. Here they built several huts out of straw, willow branches and clay. In the Portiuncula, at that time an area of meadows and marshland below the city, Francis first witnessed the establishment of the seat of the order. From then on they met here every year at Pentecost for the so-called chapter, which all of the brothers took part in, at least at the beginning. This was when all of the questions the order faced were addressed and decided. The Portiuncula would later be the model for all of the brothers' settlements. As the model settlement it was where the shared ideal was practiced in the most consistent way. When the order had already become large and popular, the citizens of the town near the Portiuncula erected a stone house to serve the large Pentecost chapter. Later when Francis arrived and saw it, he sent his brothers onto the roof to carry away the shingles and to tear the walls down. He only gave in when a declaration of the citizens stated that the building did not belong to him but to the city. Today the third largest basilica in the world stands there, but it, too, belongs to the pope. Francis had to start making concessions.

> ***Francis****: I don't know anymore exactly when I started always having to make concessions. Maybe it already began on the pilgrimage to Rome. I really thought things could just go on as they had: being dedicated to an ideal and just passionately living it out. But simple is not so simple. That was painful for me. Every possible thought shot through my mind. Should I have stayed by myself, or maintained stricter control over who joined the order? But there I go again with rules. I didn't want to regulate anything. If things had gone my way, the passion alone would have been enough.*
>
> *I already see you smiling. Now he's coming back to earth. Now reality is catching up with this oddball. Now he sees that things don't work like that. You can rest assured it got even worse. And still, every concession I had to make was painful. A piece of reality pulled me in, and it kept on that way, piece by piece. But does that ease your mind? Enthusiasm was confronted more and more with reality. Fire and ice came together. The fire warmed the ice and the ice weakened the fire. Yes, I figured it would be different. But one thing is certain: without fire you'll freeze. And in spite of everything still to come, it never went out because it didn't come only from me.*

MAKING SURE THE FIRE DIDN'T GO OUT

Francis did several things so that he never lost the fire. At the beginning he was not sure if he should withdraw from the world as a hermit to spend a solitary existence with God. He knew such experiences from the time he spent in the cave, and sometimes the thought at least entered his mind. This formed a contrast to his life as an itinerate preacher, as one who went out into the world to lead a homeless existence without a permanent residence and a roof over his head. The idea of creating an order on a large scale was something he did not imagine at that time, never mind the building of cloisters. Francis chose a mixed form. The existing hermitages give striking witness to this. He chose life in the world, but he retreated again and again for a longer time in the hermitages to replenish his inner reserves. It was clear to him that he could not always give and he did not want to face the risk of burning out. Moreover, from time to time he only wanted to belong to God and himself.

> **Francis**: *I believe places of retreat would do men good today as well. You slave away in every area of your life: for your career, your family, your hobbies, your social standing. But where is your self? If you're only driving all the time, then you run out of gas sooner or later. Who always only gives will eventually become empty. Who only tends the fire will get burned at some point. You often treat yourself pretty carelessly. What you need is less Viagra, hormones or sports programs. Much more you need places where you can get in touch with yourself.*
>
> *You need times of quiet. For many people the mere thought of this is unimaginable. And that's why it's all the*

more important. At the beginning it will be very hard and maybe even hurt. These are withdrawal symptoms, like those of an addict, and nothing else. When you give up quickly because you're cowardly or fearful, then you'll never experience the moments in life that really count. The quiet can be painful, and it has to be at first when you aren't familiar with it.

You need times of darkness. This is something many of you run away from. Life isn't made up of only what is bright and clear. It's never as simple as that. Of course it's good when you don't chase after every trivial thing or make a mountain out of a molehill. Male clarity first bears fruit when it is in balance. Everything else is just an act. But this also involves facing the darkness, and sometimes looking at what you have swept under the rug. That can hurt a lot, but you can grow and mature from it. There are so many proud peacocks and so few mature men.

You need times of want. When you don't sense your limitations, you can't deal with them. Heroes are lonely and die young. But is that what you want? It's not seldom that a lot of you don't know anymore what you want and what your own needs are. You don't have a sense of your self anymore. In reality you're the living dead. You have to learn again to listen to within, to listen to yourself, to look at what is inside you. If you don't do that, life passes you by and soon you are just left standing there like a storefront mannequin. There are already enough unhappy heroes.

Whoever is "on the air" continually can no longer receive a signal. You need places of retreat, secluded *ones at best, where you can turn off your program. From time to time you do have to question the software, but that's not possible as long as it's running. Only then do you have a chance to sense that a completely different program is running, one in which a task is set aside for you. Then the question suddenly arises: Who are you serving?*

THE REFUGE OF THE WILD MAN

The hermitages were places of retreat. They were refuges where Francis belonged only to himself and the Lord, whose service he carried out. They were places where he withdrew for prayer and contemplation, places that broke the flow of his life of activity. Here he came to peace again, plumbed anew his depths and slipped once again into the existential meaning of his life. This was something he could identify by name. Francis never wanted to have an abstract faith, nor could he. It was God, the Lord, the even greater father, who stood behind him, and it was Christ his son whose example he emulated in everything he did. In these places of retreat he immersed himself again and again in God. However, for him this was not an ecstatic act or an emptying of the self without consequence. He prayed and groaned, cheered and screamed, wept and sighed. Francis was a sensual person and what moved him inwardly also moved him outwardly. For him there was no separation.

In the hermitage Lo Speco the huge crack in the rock stretching into the earth can still be seen today. For him this was the crack that had opened in the hour of Christ's death, when the earth quaked in the third hour and rocks split open, as Scripture tells us. Francis gave himself up to the deep, mysterious womb of the earth. In the depths, where no earthly noise could penetrate and no light of day was visible, he delivered himself up to the hour of Christ's death. No person will know what he experienced there, what he opened himself up to and went through in this long night. In the other hermitages it was not much different. The brothers who were there knew they could not disturb him at this time when he led his own private life, often not coming out to eat for days.

As far as hermitages were concerned Francis knew what he wanted. Again and again he was offered places that he accepted only after first looking them over. He was very particular when he wanted to distance himself from the world. The places were always secluded on mountain peaks, but with a view of the world. A cozy dale in a valley was nothing for him. Most of the time they were lonely rocks, exposed to the elements, places of untouched nature with forests and springs. He needed water to live, and seclusion and nature brought him closer to God and God's creation. Everywhere there were caves, grottos, jutting rocks or narrow stone clefts. Because Francis often stayed in these places for weeks at a time he was thankful if a little chapel was nearby where he could pray the Liturgy of the Hours with the few brothers who were with him.

Even today these hermitages put a scratch on the prettied up pictures of the lovable Francis, Brother "Always Happy," as he was later described. They have nothing to do with the "always happy" image. They are refuges of a wild man, even if he never spoke about them much. They are places with a fascinating and at the same time oppressive atmosphere. Loneliness and peacefulness are felt here in dynamic tension with the outside world. These are rough caves Francis lived in. Here are stone slabs that he slept on and rugged stone niches where he withdrew. The thought that he was near to God in these places is both fascinating and frightening. Francis was a wild man.

> **Francis**: *I have to smile at that, but I still like to hear it. It was more often than not an experience of the wild kind and, in fact, indescribable. Today in religion the empha-*

*sis is often placed on love, niceness and shared commu-
nity. That's not wrong, but in my eyes it's not everything.
I would like to at least tell you men to have courage to
take a risk. Faith is not only a comfort but a challenge.
You can't let yourselves fall asleep in the lap of Mother
Church. Christ himself was not only loving and nice and
not only a good friend to everyone. He was also insistent,
unwavering and sometimes almost harsh in his
demands. He didn't only wash the people's feet but also
their heads.*

*Life, too, is not only soft and cushy. Sometimes it can
also wound us. Nevertheless you need to find your challenges and can't always just take the easy way out. This
is how we can grow and mature as men. Male greatness
has something both humbling and wild. It is the opposite
of brutality, which is only the compulsive aggression of
those who are inwardly weak.*

*What is wild has to take its course—from the violent
and beyond the sentimental—to finally reach a mature
form of manliness. I often experienced these stations
physically in my places of retreat for days at a time. I
could be tender because I understood nature. I loved the
birds because I knew how unyielding the earth could be.
I liked to pet the little rabbits because I knew how hard
the rocks were. I did everything for peace because I had
survived several battles, and not because I would have
been too cowardly to take them on. I could be weak
because I was strong. Only men who are inwardly weak
believe they have always to be strong; it seems they think
they don't have any other choice. It makes a difference
whether you as a man are caring and tender because life*

has made you capable of it, or because you didn't have any other choice.

Sometimes important things in life don't come automatically. In these mysterious nights in the hermitage when I gave myself up to God, I found my way to my own wildness and humility. They were crazy and indescribable hours. And some things should also remain my personal business. But I didn't only seek comfort. In essence I surrendered myself. It was no mind-expanding trip enveloped in clouds of incense, but I received an answer. I got what I needed.

T ON A NIGHT

hese were often long, quiet and lonely nights in the hermitages. Sometimes Francis lay down to rest on a stone slab and stared into the darkness. He sensed his body and, despite the cold, it seemed that someplace he was warm. Sometimes Brother Ass moved in a way he did not want. He tried to distract himself and, when nothing else worked, even used the rope from his robe to make Brother Ass think other thoughts. On a cold winter night even that did not help. Francis took off his clothes and threw himself naked onto the snow, but the cold only seemed to inflame the fire, the tinder of the flesh, as it was called at that time.

Francis rolled in the rough snow, but it did no good. He then piled snow together, forming heaps of it—one big mound of snow and four small ones. *There*, he cried aloud to himself, as he rocked back and forth, swinging his arms: *there's your wife, your two sons and two daughters. See them freezing*, he bellowed to himself, *and then make sure you can also clothe them, otherwise they'll die from exposure.* Again he threw himself on the ground in front of the piles of snow. He stood up, looked down and cried: *if just this responsibility alone is already too much for you, then don't act that way.* And so ended the nighttime episode of the naked man in the snow.

> **Francis**: *I admit that this theme isn't a very easy one for me. And still I know that sexuality is something elemental for men and that it has a lot to do with our identity. I'm afraid that I don't have much constructive advice to give you about it, not much that could be useful for you men today. I didn't exactly think about it day and night, and was just as glad when I wasn't with women too*

often. I could evade the issue a little, but naturally it was still there.

Did I fail? In a certain sense you're right if you see it that way and I would be glad to talk to you about it. That topic occupied my thoughts, even if I never really found answers that would satisfy you. How should I integrate sexuality into my life? My answers here are probably more likely helpless attempts in your eyes. I looked at those snow piles in front of me. They represented what would have been another life for me, not a less important one and one with responsibility. For me sexuality had to do with responsibility for one's reproductive nature. That helped me at least on that night as I lay naked in the snow and saw those piles of snow in front of me.

I was a person with a radical nature and I never expected everyone to lead this kind of life. On the contrary, I had a great respect for all the women and men who lived within their families and professions. There are probably many among you who can relate to these things. That's why I never would have considered trying to convince a family father to join our order. Sexuality is more important for some than for others. I probably belong to the second group, but still I was a sexual being. I never found an answer to how I could have integrated my sexuality into my one-sided radical life. That night in the snow was my attempt, though it will hardly satisfy you.

THE BROTHERS AND THEIR SISTER

The *Fratres Minores*—"Lesser Brothers"—as the order now called itself, had already grown to a substantial number when a woman knocked at their door for the first time. Clare was a bright young woman, just eighteen, sophisticated and from a house of good standing. Her family lived in a palace on the cathedral square. Her cousin had already joined the Order of Friars Minor two years before, though the topic had not been a subject of conversation in the House Favarone since that time. Clare was often able to observe Francis and his brothers when they appeared in town, and at some point the idea dawned on her: Why couldn't there also be an order of minor sisters?

She asked her cousin to intervene and thus several secret meetings took place between her and Francis. They were not secret because there was anything to hide. After all, a confidante of her house was always with them. They were secret because her reputation was at stake and because her leave-taking would have to be arranged with the utmost caution. In the night before Palm Sunday 1212, when Francis had reached the age of thirty, the time had come. There was a pious conspiracy of the women in the Favarone household, because at that time a girl could not just simply walk out of the town at night unnoticed. She got out of the house with difficulty by way of a rear exit. Presumably the night watchman was also initiated, as the Portiuncula lay far outside the city walls, which were locked at night.

In any case, somehow she made it there and now stood at the door requesting admission. Francis cut off her hair as a sign of her profession. Now the brothers had a sister. Wonderful, one might say, but it was not as simple as that. A lone woman among men would have been even more frowned on at that time than today. Francis' relationship with women was not exactly unproblematic either, but it had to do with more than that. While men could easily place themselves on the side of the poor and downtrodden, for a woman it was an entirely different matter. Even when Clare might have imagined for herself a life similar to that of the brothers, it would have been a far too dangerous undertaking for her as a woman. Francis had tried to make this clear to her in some of the discussions following her admission. And the brother seemed to be at a loss.

Whatever the case may be, Clare was brought to the nearby cloister of Benedictine nuns in the early morning hours. In the meantime her disappearance had been noticed in the Favarone house, and a delegation of relatives—strangely enough there is never any mention of her father—set out in search of her. One of the maidservants apparently provided the answer to her whereabouts. When the relatives found Clare in the aforementioned cloister and wanted to take her home with them, she revealed to them the sign of her profession: her shorn head. The group then retreated a short time later without any signs of violence. There must have been something special about the women (and men?) of this house, as Clare's sister Agnes followed her two weeks later, and one after another almost the entire female household joined the order, her sisters, the ladies-in-waiting and finally even her mother.

There were problems in the cloister and, after all, Clare had not chosen to become a Benedictine nun. Francis had in fact taken her into his own order. He had to find a solution and turned to the Bishop of Assisi, who provided him with the chapel of San Damiano. In a short period of time, the brothers built a cloister there for the women. The former living quarters of the priest was renovated and a sleeping area was built for the sisters over the church, which now had a secure foundation. In this isolated place the Poor Ladies of San Damiano, as they were known from then on, lived a life of poverty, in seclusion from the world. Sister Clare, who died in 1253 at age fifty-nine, spent the rest of her life behind the walls of the cloister. Shortly before her death, when she was already very ill, Clare felt compelled to steadfastly assert the Rule of her order, when the pope would have wished for less severity. Clare was consistent, no less radical and undoubtedly obedient as well. Was this the life the young woman had dreamt of? Many questions must simply remain unanswered.

> **Francis**: *That was a sensitive matter, and one that's not simple for me to explain. Naturally, it's easy for you to talk today. First, it was truly a moment of great happiness when a woman wanted to enter our way of life for the first time. And it was only a matter of time before more women would follow. We were without a doubt very proud that there was now a female branch of our order. The question of whether or not Clare had imagined how things would turn out is a reasonable one. I probably don't have a satisfactory answer for modern-day women, and still I don't know what I could have done differently. This is something I just have to live with.*
>
> *We were a community of men and that was important. It's still the same scenario today: a group of men is together peacefully and as soon as a woman joins them the discord begins. At the same time, it's not the woman's fault. The life we chose was also one without women. But we still had great respect for every man who was married*

and had a family. And we also had respect for women. But one can't have everything at the same time. Some things in life eliminate others and then you are forced to make a decision. We made a decision. By the way, the women of our order placed just as much importance on being strictly among themselves later. I don't know if you can understand that.

Clare was a self-confident, lively person. Her steadfast decision to live the life of the poor would have been a hard pill for anyone else to swallow. When she announced her decision her face was radiant. Her eyes lit up and sparkled when she spoke about my role as model for her and what I had done with my life. Maybe women are captivated by something in a more holistic way—for want of a better way to put it. Not that there was anything suggestive about her behavior, but as a man you never know. I was overjoyed, but nevertheless felt I should distance myself a bit. She would never have understood my problem, and maybe even would have been a little suspicious. But I needed a little while until I could find brotherly clarity again with respect to my enraptured sister. With borders respect can also grow.

ACROSS THE ALPS AND BACK

The order expanded on a great scale in Italy, and at some point the question arose about whether the brothers should cross the borders of present-day Italy to the north across the Alps and south across the sea. They agreed on this mission at the Pentecost chapter of 1217, when Francis was thirty-five years old. It was a risky venture for which they were little prepared, but they undertook it out of deep conviction and with great passion. One danger that faced them was the threat of being confused with one of the sectarian groups traveling north and west of the Alps. Although they were well known in Italy, in other countries the brothers were not always easy to identify. In France they were promptly stopped on the assumption that they belonged to a sect. However, the one who stopped them was a bishop who knew Latin. The brothers presented him with the Rule as it stood up to that time, having only received verbal approval by the pope. They were taken into custody while an enquiry was made. A few weeks later a papal confirmation was received stating that the brothers were thoroughly Catholic.

In Hungary they were treated even worse. On the wide plains of the Puszta they ran up against shepherds who taunted them with skewers. In their trusting nature—they could not understand a single word—they thought the shepherds were after their robes. They also wore pants and underwear beneath them in the northern regions. One by one they handed these over to the shepherds until they were left standing there with nothing on. But the shepherds still did not let up. A brother who had already lost his underwear six times this way thought this must in fact be what they were after. In desperation he smeared his underpants with ox manure so he would be spared them. The shepherds became queasy from the stench and soon stopped their harassment. Nevertheless, the brothers soon decided to leave this country and returned to Italy again.

For a long time Germany was an especially feared place among the brothers because of what had taken place there. Not a single one of them was versed in the language, but somehow they learned the word *ja*—"yes." When the people saw the penniless brothers and asked them if they needed food and shelter, they always answered *ja*. This approach functioned very well for a time, and they thought they had found the magic word. One day, however, they were asked if they were members of a sect from Lombardy who wanted to infiltrate Germany. They happily replied *ja*. At this, they were beaten, locked up and led naked into the marketplace where they were made a public spectacle. They recouped as quickly as possible and fled back to Italy. After that time Germany was considered an especially terrible land for the brothers.

A few years later, in spite of resistance, the order set forth in a new attempt to cross into Germany, only this time with the German brother Caesar of Speyer at the helm of the undertaking. He had stayed on in Palestine following one of the Crusades and joined the order of the Lesser Brothers there. With difficulty they succeeded in crossing the Brenner and were also successful in entering Tyrolia. To everyone's delight the first German they met in the country, a short distance from present-day Garmisch, wanted to join the order. This was a good sign. Unfortunately, he had a name that was unpronounceable for the Italians. Thus Brother Hartmut was rechristened Brother Andrew.

The brothers who were sent out to the Arab Muslims, the Saracens, had the worst time of it. With great difficulty the brothers were able to make their way across France to Spain and from there to Morocco, where they were imprisoned and executed. These were the first brothers who died as martyrs, men who gave their lives for their conviction.

Francis: When I think about it today I still feel uneasy. You'll laugh at some of what these greenhorns had to put up with. No question about it, this mission wasn't thought out from A to Z, but was totally unplanned. And why not? Our community had experienced growth at an unparalleled pace. The number of brothers grew from day to day, and at the same time we became ever more popular in central Italy. We had public and official support, and it wasn't seldom that we were met with downright enthusiasm. The question of whether we should bring our message to other countries was only natural. The assumption that conditions would be similar was of course completely without thought and very naive. We were simply too full of excitement.

Naturally I am still shaken today to think of how unprepared and lacking in any foreign language skills these brothers were. I feel very sorry for those who suffered as a consequence. Yet I still stand by what we did. Risk-taking is a part of life, even when it isn't so naive. "Nothing ventured, nothing gained" is an old saying, and a valid one. Security isn't unimportant, but it cannot be our only standard in life. There is more involved. That's why we have to dare to take a risk. What is in fact a setback if not proof that something was attempted?

We were passionate and we had a directive. We also made mistakes. But isn't it worse to stagnate somewhere along the way drained of inspiration? Is it really better to risk nothing than to risk making mistakes? My personal answer remains clear. Whoever is only looking for security suffocates in it. Without taking a risk we cannot change. Men without courage are only bringers of doom and gloom. They no longer radiate anything and at some point just dry up. They are the living dead.

THE END OF A HERO'S JOURNEY

What had happened to the martyrs left a lasting impression on Francis. He was tortured by his guilty conscience because of his brothers who had been killed on their mission in Morocco. On the other hand, the emotional fever of the Crusades had broken out at that time and many young men were attracted by the lure of the East, where they could quickly become knights. Francis had long ago ended this chapter in his life, yet a new heroism took root within him when he decided to travel to the East himself two years later with the not very humble intention of evangelizing the sultan. After the double-edged success that he had already experienced, this decision was undoubtedly based on a wish to accomplish something great once more, even if it meant dying as a martyr like his fellow brothers. He at least wanted to know that he had tried.

Following the Pentecost chapter of 1219, Francis departed, at the age of thirty-seven, and by ship and on foot, two months later reached Damietta in Egypt. Arabs occupied the holy sites in Palestine—the reason the pope had strictly forbidden entering them—while battles raged in Egypt between Christian crusaders and the sultan's men. Francis burst onto the scene of these battles following his arrival and experienced the anguish of the Christian crusaders' defeat. What he saw spurred him on all the more in his desire for peace.

One month later as the battles flamed up again, he crossed the enemy lines, barefoot and in his gray robe, with the tenacity of the steadfast. The Arabs tortured and beat the strange man, who was not fluent in their language and continually cried out in his poor pronunciation: *Soldan! Soldan!* He was an odd sight to be sure, and yet they were not able to cause him any real harm and after a while let up. Maybe it was again the fervor in his eyes and the peaceful smile that irritated them. After various ordeals, he was in fact finally brought before the sultan whom he had wanted to see so badly.

Sultan Melek-el-Kamel was a highly learned man and in no way a wild animal, as the Saracens were commonly characterized. The reception was by all accounts conducted with honor. Even though the sultan acknowledged the peaceful objective, the meeting itself remained without success. The language barrier alone put the men in two entirely different worlds. Francis did not fail for lack of courage, but it seemed he had indeed imagined his undertaking to be easier than it was. After a few days, the sultan had Francis brought back to the Christian army under military escort. What Francis was forced to witness shortly after this encounter was much worse than anything he had seen up to that time. At the beginning of November the Christian crusaders conquered Damietta and carried out a truly un-Christian bloodbath there. Of the 80,000 residents of the city, only 3,000 would survive the inferno. Francis had previously heard stories about the cruelty of the Saracens, but what he saw from his own troops outdid anything he could imagine. The cruelty of the Christian army shook the ideals of every pious crusader to its foundation. Everything had come about so differently than he ever could have imagined.

The journey to the East was a serious personal blow for Francis in every way, and the consequences were significant. This was not the high point in life he had dreamt of. In fact, just the opposite: the knight of Christ, who aspired to fight for peace with the Word and the service of his life was left with nothing.

He neither succeeded in converting the sultan nor did he die the heroic death of a martyr. Instead he was forced to be a helpless witness to the brutality of the Christian crusaders. And not that he cared much about Brother Ass, but on this trip he also caught malaria and a painful eye infection, from which he suffered the rest of his life.

> **Francis**: *I wanted to try again, not only just ministering to what had been achieved, or living from my fame, but I wanted to sense myself again, to stand on the frontlines and accomplish something great. This was also at an age when the middle of life is reached, when the biological curve inevitably takes a turn. I think I wanted to prove something again. And then everything came so differently from what I had imagined. And it was terrible. Blow after blow rained down on me like waves. The last remnants of heroism fell away like the dust of ashes. Was this all and was it how the great Francis should end? Questions filled my head and it was like someone had pulled the rug out from under my feet. I fell into a hole. The waves seemed to crash down over me, blocking the way to the light forever.*
>
> *It was my midlife crisis, even if I would not live as long as you today. I see it as a painful time of change, which finally led to something new. Today I know that this phase was important and necessary. There can be no rise without a fall, and the fall began at this time. In this moment, however, I only felt hurt, numb and hopeless. The dismal hole was gloomy and dark. The vitality, the open expression of courage and my will to fight—it was all over. I had to withstand so many trials by fire,*

had to prove myself in so many ways, and would never have thought the worst was yet to come. I was convinced that things would just continue as they had been going and success would follow success. That was the youthful dream of the hero. But the ladder of success didn't lead to heaven—it stopped at the ceiling.

It was the worst thing that could happen to me. The earlier hurdles could be cleared by the power of will, and beyond I just kept going on, forward and up. This was over. Power and effort no longer did any good. Many things were irreversible up to that point and there was no going back. But the wounds that life inflicts on us have their purpose. It was the beginning of the descent, the beginning of the transformation: from the spotlight to the inner self, from pridefulness to humility, from success to inner maturation, from growth and struggle to seasoned fruit in the hand of the Lord.

THE OVERTAXED HEN

One might think there had been enough setbacks, but events continued to take unexpected turns. When Francis traveled across the ocean to Egypt, together with Peter di Cantanio, he left two surrogates behind to keep an eye on things. While in the East he was met one day by a brother who had left Italy without permission, in order to report to Francis what was taking place in his absence. Things must have been in a mess. At one chapter they tried, said the loyal brother almost out of breath, to make the fasting regulations stricter and change the Rule to suit the members of the order present. He had indeed come without permission, the brother declared, and he hoped his mild father would forgive him, but the surrogates were causing chaos throughout the entire order in Italy.

They were sitting at the table and meat had just been served, as the brother dug out the new decree with the stricter fasting regulations and placed it before the founder of the order. Francis turned to Peter and innocently asked what they should do. Peter carefully returned the question to Francis, who after all was the one with the authority. A big grin appeared on Francis' face as he quoted a passage from the Gospels, which Peter knew as well as he did: When a person comes into a city and is invited into a house, he eats what is put before him. What he then said was celebrated with no less pleasure: Therefore let us eat what has been set in front of us according to the Gospel. Francis was not exactly a comic, but often this side of his nature revealed itself when there was otherwise nothing left to laugh about. In any case, the "runaway brother" let out a sigh of relief. At the first opportunity, Francis set off for Italy with several brothers, not to the Portiuncula but to the pope in Rome. Humbly he squatted before the pope's door and waited for him to come out. Once before the pope he revoked all of the decrees put through by his representatives. At the same time he asked if he could be granted a cardinal protector—an official protector of the order: *Give me someone I can consult when necessary, who will listen to the matters of my order in your stead and attend to them.* All of this was starting to be more than he could cope with.

One night Francis had a dream that again reflected his situation visually. He saw a little black hen that had so many chicks she was no longer able to shelter them all under her wings. More and more chicks had to stay outside, and were running around the hen wildly. The dream hit the nail on the head. There were too many brothers. The wings were his personal example that had guided the brothers up to now. It was a loathsome thought for Francis to imagine himself parading around as the boss or setting up comprehensive rules. The gospel, the inner passion and the shared vitality should have been enough. The little hen had painfully to see that these times were over.

> **Francis**: *This situation was in fact more than I could cope with. And it wasn't what I wanted. I wasn't the born leader type or someone who wanted sovereignty. Some men can do that very well when they are a little older, milder and more mature. Then they no longer react by waving around a scepter, but deal with things out of an inner instinct. They recognize what's wrong, what's needed and show concern for those entrusted to their care without even having to do a lot. It's enough when they're present and take their place. Everything runs smoothly and everyone feels comfortable. That wasn't my gift. I was not the born superior of an order.*

Then there are those who are simply born doers. They have a good overview and know what counts so that everything functions well. They have the ability to organize and to think about ten things at once. They know how to cleverly pull the strings, to look into the future and to take the necessary measures. These things have always held a fascination for me as a trained merchant, but they weren't my personal strength.

I was a fighter and a lover, if you understand what I mean. I wanted to fight for the gospel, for the poor and the oppressed, and for peace. This was the knight coming through. I wanted to fight for great ideals—for nothing less than the Good News of God. But in my heart it went against my grain to fight in order that my own brothers followed the Rule, or to worry about tying up all the organizational loose ends. I wouldn't have been a good superior; I was much too impatient and intolerant. I probably would have always had a club in my hand.

But I withdrew more and more when a brother didn't fulfill my expectations. This wasn't only a gesture of humility but also of self-protection. When somebody got on my nerves, I went to pray. And that was the lover. When I could withdraw to a quiet place, somewhere in nature, with birds around me, then I was very close to myself and close to God. Then it just didn't interest me anymore who said what, or how something was supposed to be done. These were the happy moments in my last years of life. I felt my limitations and, at the same time, had painfully to recognize that all of these things were still necessary. I really felt just like that little hen. What was once so beautiful was over forever. The hole opened again and I groped my way along in the darkness using my limitations to guide me. It was like I had reached the end of a flagpole, and only when I recognized this could I find support.

THE DESCENT TO PERFECT JOY

The little hen exited the stage. At the next Pentecost chapter, when Francis was thirty-eight years old, to everyone's surprise, he gave up full leadership of the order. The dramatic words preceding the announcement of his decision contained much of the personal hurt that lay behind him. *In the future I am a dead man for you,* Francis said. At this time he also introduced the new general minister, Peter di Cantanio, whom all brothers, including himself, were to obey in the future. To emphasize this he bowed before Brother Peter as a sign of deference.

The brothers were horrified. No one had been expecting this. The overall unhappiness that followed was for some undoubtedly mixed with a guilty conscience. The formal relinquishment of the order's leadership was, however, more than inner resignation. Once again Francis was holding up a mirror before his brothers. He did not get into a discussion regarding his decision, as there was nothing to discuss. He took action and that was that. This was surely all the more reason for the brothers to pursue the issue further. Questions remained they had to figure out themselves, and yet through his actions he had already given them the answer.

Several months later Peter di Cantanio died, and at the following Pentecost chapter Francis designated Elias of Cortona as his successor. The title "minister" general might sound a bit pretentious to our ears today, but at that time Latin was the language in use and in Latin *minister* means nothing other than "servant." In addition to the minister general, there were other ministers who were responsible for the leadership of the order in their respective provinces in Europe and the East. When it was no longer possible for all the brothers of the order to meet at the Portiuncula, it was the provincial ministers in particular who met there once a year on Pentecost.

Even if Francis had given up the official leadership and declared his obedience to the respective superior, he remained the spiritual authority. On one occasion when he was sitting at the feet of the minister general, he tugged at his robe. Elias bent down, asked what he wished and then announced it to the others: *Brothers, thus speaks the brother*. However, if the interpretation and following of the Rule were involved, then Francis was always the final authority. He just did not want to have to struggle with it anymore, although he was still not spared of this entirely. With the expansion of the order over the years, new questions continually came up which were clarified at the Pentecost chapters. Year after year, further resolutions and regulations were added to the original Rule of the order approved by Pope Innocent III. These were pragmatic adaptations to new and different circumstances. For Francis they were bothersome matters of necessity and he would have preferred that they had not been needed. In the meantime, the number of members had increased at such a rapid rate Francis could no longer keep track of them, and he was forced again to do something that did not fit into his scheme of things. It was necessary to compose a comprehensive Rule of the Order with the purpose of presenting it again to the pope, this time for written approval.

Lateran Council IV of 1215 had deemed that new orders were to adapt themselves to the rules of existing orders. The cardinal protector now tried, supported by the more conformist brothers, to push one of these rules on Francis. But this did not even come into question. It was primarily the learned brothers who were behind this idea, and Elias, the pragmatist, probably speculated about it as well. Francis had never been a conformist, nor did his way of thinking have much to do with pragmatism. Further, he lacked higher education. What he had was an explicit directive, and it was crystal clear to him who gave him his instructions. Once again he had to fight for things that were, for Francis, not open to discussion. He fought and became forceful.

The cardinal and the aforementioned brothers presented him with the Rule of Bernhard, Benedict and Augustine in the hope that he might still allow himself to be led by them. The cardinal himself used the brothers to back him up when he advised Francis to follow their wise advice. Francis did not mince words. God himself and no one else had shown him this way of simplicity. There was no mention of Benedict or Bernard or anyone else. The instructions given to him by the Lord were that he should be a *new fool in the world.* And, in words directed to the scholars, he said that God would give these wise guys what was coming to them. That hit home. The cardinal was silent and the brothers trembled in consternation.

Francis would rather have been the hen that gathered the chicks under her wings than to impose a new rule, but he was not spared this. Together with a brother who was well versed in the Bible, he set to work. He combined the original Rule with the later resolutions and added spiritual admonitions. It was the duty of the brother who assisted him to include quotations from the Bible throughout the entire text so that its relation to the gospel would be presented even more clearly. The conclusion was powerful: *I order that no one is to delete what is written in this dictate, nor add anything to it in written form, and additionally that the brothers should have no other Rule.* The conclusion reflected not only the necessity of the new Rule, but also the power of that which was contained in it.

After the completion of this work, Francis set off on another preaching journey through Italy in order to serve again finally the One for whom he was really there. Much to his vexation the matter was not over, since the new pope refused to grant his approval to the Rule now placed before him. The refusal was, however, not just a stumbling block put in Francis' way by the official church but had—once again—a reasonable basis. The second Rule was certainly well meant, but, for its purpose, it simply did not cover enough. It was too long, too much like a sermon, not juristic enough. A third of the work consisted of quotations from the Bible, as if the man from Assisi had cornered the market on the Gospels—some in Rome probably would have thought. Francis had tried to compose a spiritual text that he could live with, a text that expressed his mentality and was exactly for this reason not a legal set of rules. Once more what was required was precisely what he did not want. Almost two years later he retreated for better or worse to the hermitage Fonte Colombo, to do just what should not have been necessary in his eyes. Influential brothers continued to exert pressure in the background for fear the Rule might end up being too strict. Presumably the minister general, Brother Elias, was also involved. Not that Francis let himself be talked into anything, but it was a laborious and undoubtedly unwelcome work, in which he had support from the legal experts of the Roman Curia. Nonetheless, in the same year, one month before Christmas 1223, Pope Honorius II affirmed the final Rule. Francis could undoubtedly still look at himself in the mirror, but the visionary inside him was tormented by the constraints of what was feasible and the pained idealist by every compromise. In Fonte Colombo he often thought about the past with longing.

In these years Francis increasingly withdrew from the public eye and spent more and more time in his hermitages. Only his closest brothers were with him, most of them from earlier times. He was dependent on their companionship, if only because he was in reality very sick. The malaria continued to plague him and his eyes watered and hurt, and on the whole he had not treated Brother Ass very well. The hermitages had always been his places of retreat for periods of time, but now they increasingly became an important retreat from the order, from a development he could not stop, from all the changes and compromises, from the many practical necessities and also from the demanding fervor that came at him from all sides. The places of retreat became his places of flight in the final, painful years of his life.

> **Francis**: *Talking about the events of these years is difficult. It was a painful path that, in its own way, led me to myself. It was the road leading downward that I had to take and I did. It was the wounds life inflicted on me. But the path led me to what was essential, only of a different nature than I had dreamed. Nothing more was dreamlike, but for me this was the time of my greatest maturation. It belonged to me and I belonged to myself as I had not for a long time. But that still doesn't change anything about my frailty.*
>
> *For me it was a time of inwardness. There were very personal things that were important to me in the last years of my life. Very little time remained for me. It's not easy for me to describe this and there are some things I would like to keep for myself. There were phases when the joy truly disappeared. And that was when I sunk into my hole of depression. Handing over the order was a step*

that I personally took and it did me good. It was an important and active step, not just one of desperation. Suddenly I had something to hold on to, ground under my feet and it made me free. But then all the fuss started with the Rule of the order and I could not let this cup pass me by. Even when it sometimes cost me all my strength, I would have been denying myself had I not accepted this ordeal.

Again and again I asked myself where the joy was that had filled me, even when I embraced the leper. One night I dictated a story to Brother Leo, who was very close to me and who was with me most of the time in my final years. I asked him if he knew what true and complete joy was. He shrugged his shoulders and picked up the writing instrument with deliberation. I had an idea, a bright and unexpected light in the darkness. It had followed me for weeks but had remained somehow diffuse. When I turned to Brother Leo it became clearer, and then came word for word.

Write, I told him, if all the professors at the universities in Paris joined our order it is not true joy. Leo's feather scratched away so quickly he didn't even have time to think about it. And if all the abbots, prelates and bishops in Germany, France and England were to join our order, this is not true joy. Brother Leo sighed, because he could hardly keep up writing, and from time to time it almost sounded like some sighs of exasperation were mixed in. And if the King of France, I continued to dictate, and the King of England joined our order, it is not true joy. Leo wrote and wrote and, as if he thought I wouldn't see him, slightly rolled his eyes. And if our *brothers even evangelized the Muslims . . . Brother Leo guessed what was coming and continued to write. And if I could heal the sick and perform miracles with the grace of God like Jesus, it is not true joy. Leo seemed close to desperation.*

What then is true joy? he cried out in despair. When late on a winter night, I arrive at the Portiuncula from a long journey, dirty and frozen through, ice on the hem of the robe flapping against my bloody shins . . . Leo looked at me with big, questioning eyes. When I then come to the gate, and knock and after a long time a brother looks through the crack in the door and asks who is there, and I answer Brother Francis, and . . . Leo could hardly keep up with writing. . . . the brother then answers, Go back to where you came from, no one goes out at this time of night. You can't come in. And then when I once more beg for entry and the brother still remains unmoved and sends me away a second time . . . Leo could hardly catch his breath and I gave him a break so he could at least catch up. He stared at me when he was ready and waited for the answer. I say to you, Brother Leo, if I then keep patient and don't get upset, then this is true and complete joy. Leo could hardly write anymore.

Maybe that's the craziest thought I had ever had in my crazy life. For me, too, this thought was only the direction, a path I was only sometimes able to take myself. But I had these moments of true joy. And they cannot be compared to the earlier happiness resulting from something that had turned out to be successful. It was a place that I first had to reach. Open yourself to this crazy experiment sometime. It can make you inwardly free.

The moments of true joy, as I experienced them, are the restfulness of the spirit and the peace of the heart, entirely independent of outward circumstances. It is the freedom you experience when you let go of the outside situation. Maybe it's not a message for young men who have the ascent before them, but it can be a way for men who are in the middle of their life, and like me are suddenly faced with the question: Was that all? It can be a direction for men who sense all at once that success, recognition, status, popularity and power are not the true sources of joy—that one day these things suddenly no longer sustain you.

In our eagerness, we sometimes re-create what life is really all about and then just get stuck in that place. Then one day comes a painful awakening: injustice and the reward that never came for our personal performance. Most of the time we then perform even more because, after all, doesn't life have to be fair in the end? But who ever said that life was fair? We make up this fiction ourselves. Life is life and sometimes it is put together backward. Some fall into self-pity because of this, accusing the world or other people, looking for someone else to take the blame. Then on top of it they might even meet someone who announces that you always have to feel good and then proceed to try out every ridiculous thing possible which doesn't do any good or only serves as a temporary distraction.

In the middle of life, at the latest, we men realize, if we're honest, that things can't always be in upward motion, that performance and success aren't everything, that the pattern of life is woven backward, forward, every which way and also has its holes. We can then either mature from it, despair because of it or nonchalantly swagger through it.

Maturing always means being able to recognize what is happening around us as well. But the world is not there only so that we can do well in it. We are a part of it, and the earth does not revolve around only us. The way to true joy, as I have described it, is only a direction, not a recipe for success. But following the way to true joy is better than hanging on to something without substance.

During those days it became clear to me that I would have to say goodbye to many things. The attempted evangelization of the non-Christians, including the sultan, was not my true source of joy, nor was the immense expansion of the order, the high standing in the church and among the population, nor the responsible leadership of a great community and, least of all, not the admiration from my own brothers. What I experienced in the last years of my life, despite my time of illness, were my completely personal moments of deep happiness. It was not the visions I had imagined in the eagerness of my youth, but it was that which truly made the end of my life a happy one.

THE MAN AND THE CHILD

At the end of the year 1223, when he was about forty-two years old, Francis invented the Christmas celebration at the hermitage in Greccio. Not that before this time there was no Christmas, but the form we have goes back to him. Without him there would be no crèche, no celebrations of the Nativity and Christmas would probably not be the high point in people's lives that it is, even when learned theologians never tire of declaring that Easter, the celebration of the Resurrection, is the highest feast day. They are not wrong, but still . . .

Three years before this time Francis had given up leadership of the order, and just a few weeks before the pope had approved the final Rule. These things were thus taken care of. Francis was already very sick and he could only sleep sitting up because of his eyes. He had always loved Greccio because here among the simple people he found the resonance he missed in some of his brothers. The village was situated on a hill above the Rieti Valley, a half-hour's walk from the hermitage, wedged into a rocky area above the valley. People from Greccio often came over to the hermitage in the evening to sing Vespers with the brothers. Here Francis felt at home.

What he had planned in Greccio was not a spontaneous happening but well thought out. He entrusted a pious man from the village named John with the preparations. He wanted—three years before his death—to celebrate Christmas in a special way. He wanted to make the foundation of his life visible. Francis was a sensual, concrete person, who wanted to see, sense and experience what he believed in. For him this meant Christ as God incarnate, and he wanted, as he said, to make him as tangible as possible for human eyes, because, after all, he was human. Francis was naive in the best sense of the word. Dry theories and abstract thought were not of much use to him. What he believed in had once possessed a form, and must take on a form again.

The day was at hand. Many brothers came from other settlements. The men and women streamed in with torches and candles. Francis had seen to it that everything was prepared. There was a manger with hay and an ox and donkey on either side. In the glow of the fire the people brought with them, the night became as bright as day. They sang and the rocks above the hermitage echoed with their voices. A priest celebrated Mass while Francis stood by the manger in tears, as the brothers sang at the top of their lungs. Francis read the Gospel in his melodious voice. It carried him away and in a flowing transition he proceeded to preach to the people. When he spoke about the Christ-child, it was as if he were savoring the name itself on his tongue. He proclaimed the word Bethlehem with the fervor of a bleating lamb. He was beside himself. The chorus of song echoed again and again, and it was a long time before the celebration was over and the people returned to their homes full of blessed joyfulness.

In this way our Christmas celebrations began. The night in Greccio was a religious performance. For Francis it did not have to do with a spiritual or even cosmic Christ, but one, who in his own words became so tangible that he could see him with his own eyes. In light of all the starkness in his life, he did not shy away from this expression of an emotional-sensory sign of his faith. Francis countered the structure of theology with religious feeling and experience. He wanted to physically see, sense and live out what he believed in. He wanted Jesus to literally melt on his tongue.

Once, when Christmas fell on a Friday, normally a day when meat was forbidden, a few brothers worried about how Francis might react, hoping he would not go too far. An especially motivated brother turned to Francis diligently and cautiously said that Christmas, however, did fall on a Friday this year, and after all this did mean that no meat could be eaten, didn't it? Francis broke in, *Brother, you are sinning if you call this day Friday.* And he proclaimed ceremoniously at the same time, *On this day I even want the walls to eat meat, and if they can't they should at least be spread with it!* For Francis there were no compromises when it came to Christmas.

As much as the crucified Christ and his suffering held a central place for him, in Greccio Francis bridged a link to the birth of the Lord. In response to a brother who asked him about this, he answered that the Lord would never have been able to redeem us if he had not been born. His thanks and understanding were focused on the incarnate Christ, and it was clear to Francis that birth and death belong together in life. The child, whose birth he recreated that night, became increasingly important to Francis as he aged. What he celebrated on this night was for him a personal matter of the heart. The brothers who were there and the people of Greccio were a part of this joy. Greccio was far away from the Portiuncula. Francis was completely one with himself.

> **Francis**: *The sensory part of faith was always important to me. "Enlightened" men will have their trouble with that, but abstract things were always too little for me. Grown men sometimes cry at Christmas, even if they then suddenly don't know what to do or have a few drinks to hide it. After the emotion follows embarrassment. But in Scriptures it says we are to become like little children.*

When we don't care for the child in us we'll get old too fast. Why shouldn't our faith also take on a childlike, naive form? I could never find sustenance in dry talk and discussion. Some men should, without a doubt, climb down from their lofty throne of reason from time to time. They would then experience something completely new. Why is it that especially when it comes to anything religious men are so often afraid?

Many men have difficulties anyway with emotions. Although they feel this elemental force in themselves, they can't categorize it. And that makes them afraid. They fear they can't control their feelings, not to mention losing the control over themselves. That would probably be the worst thing they could imagine. As a result, everything is cemented over or buried. But I don't mean emotional gushing either. Not all feelings are the same and even tears can lie. That much is clear to me. When men listen to themselves they will be able to recognize the difference well. After all, anger and rage are feelings, too, even when some people act as if these feelings are not legitimate because they aren't very nice. Wounds and hurt are important sensations that men should take seriously. The question is not whether they are agreeable or welcome but whether they are real.

Reason alone is not the whole man by a long shot. Men with feelings, not whining emotional gushers, convey reassuring warmth. They radiate emotional reassurance and security. They know how to deal with their feelings, but are also able to just let themselves go sometimes. In doing this they only win without losing anything. Men who always keep their feelings under lock *and key dry up at some point. Sooner or later they become alien to themselves and cut themselves off from the living. They have no emotional access to what they do and, when it comes right down to it, don't know what to do with themselves anymore. When men make a detour around feelings and sensations, it is false self-protection. They no longer get what they need when they cover everything up with a cement of strength. They protect themselves from what could help them. Maybe it's similar with religion. "Real men" think they have to make an especially wide detour around it. That's just something for weaklings, or for those in need. The man is in and of himself complete, what does he need others for? A lot of men have the fear of no longer being in control. But that's actually how life is. We can't control everything. If we try we'll be crushed. At the same time we always remain the child and are always needy. Happy is the man who knows this. He doesn't end up too short, and he knows that he can give himself up to the flow of life, not to mention the flow of the even Greater One.*

HANDS AND FEET IN PAIN

Many years before this time, Count Orlando of Chisui, after witnessing Francis give a passionate sermon, had given him his great object of admiration: the mountain of La Verna. It was intended as a place of hermitage. As previously mentioned, Francis was very particular when it came to his places of retreat. He first had two brothers check to see if this site would be suitable. It was.

La Verna is situated high in the mountains of northern Tuscany, near the source of the Tiber and Arno rivers. A rough stone projection near this place separates the two creeks before they become the legendary rivers. Below Mount Penna there is a rock ledge, near the precipice, above the path the inhabitants take with their mules. Far away from the world in dizzying heights is the rock encircled by clouds. Every idyllic image ends here, for the weather can change from hour to hour on the mountain. Unpredictable and fascinating, La Verna was a place Francis yearned for at this time in his life. Here he was far away from the order, from the public, from Rome, from everything that forced him to do things he did not want to do.

In the late summer of 1224, when Francis was forty-two, he withdrew to this mountain at the time of the so-called Lent of Saint Michael. The occasion was actually more of a pretext, as he yearned for quiet, peace and seclusion. Here in the heights of the mountain no one disturbed him. Here he was alone, in the middle of nature and here he hoped anew to experience the closeness of God's presence. Thus, what Francis experienced and lived through on La Verna is all the more his personal matter and does not deserve to be dragged into the light of speculation. This was done enough by others after his death.

At the end of August, he withdrew here to the coolness and seclusion of his hermitage. Two or three brothers lived there, and Brother Leo, who was especially close to him, accompanied him. They had built themselves simple huts out of boards and branches. Leo sat for hours, days and nights above on the rocks, while Francis devoted himself to his contemplation below under a rock overhang.

Leo could have almost given up. He was going through a tough time himself, dealing with personal doubts, and had hoped for supportive dialogue. He was looking forward to the time together with Francis, and now he would have nothing from it. From time to time he was allowed to bring him water and something to eat, and then only when a special signal was given. It was not unusual for Francis to forget to eat. Francis was in seclusion for himself. And just when Leo could have used his help.

Francis still sensed this, because he was close to Leo. One day he gave him a small piece of parchment paper, on which he had written a blessing from the Old Testament: *The Lord bless and protect you. May his face shine upon you and grant you mercy. May he turn his face toward you and give you peace.* A little below this Francis had written: *The Lord bless you, Brother Leo.* On the back of the parchment Leo found a hymn of praise to God—the euphoric profession of one in love with God. He folded the paper and fixed it inside his robe where he carried the parchment with him until the end of his life. Leo was going through a crisis and especially in need during these days in La Verna. If his brother was not available to him, at least he had this comforting piece of paper.

Francis lay for days and nights on a rock, deep in contem-

plation of the Passion of Christ. After a Christmas in Greccio
rich with sensory images, his focus was now on the other side.
And this other side for Francis should not be any less concrete
than the first. For days at a time he hardly ate anything and
appeared less frequently to join the others in praying the Liturgy
of the Hours. It was clear to the brothers that they had to leave
him in his solitude. These were long, lonely, intense days and
nights Francis spent on La Verna, times when he also experienced visions. Now he was reliant on himself, but in a different
way than in the early years. He met the Crucified One another
time, but this time he was no longer renovating churches. This
time it was his personal, inner experience.

Francis received the stigmata of the Lord, and we will leave
it at that. Skeptics and voyeurs often hone in on this event, carrying it to extremes. So, too, in a different way, do members of
his own order, beginning with Brother Elias. What happened on
La Verna concerned Francis alone. And that is how he wanted it
to be treated. Until his death there was hardly a brother who saw
the wounds of the stigmata, and Francis did everything to hide
them. The events on La Verna were his own personal act, neither
exemplary nor useful for others, as he said. Even in the records
of his canonization they do not surface. The church always had
a grounded instinct in such matters. Such records could become
another form of machinery that sensationalized the fact.

In his vision an angel with six wings appeared to him, and in
the middle of the wings the Crucified One was revealed. Two
wings were spread in flight, two were raised to heaven and two
covered the body of the Crucified One. Francis was in total rap-
ture. He saw the beauty of the vision and he saw the passion of
the crucified Lord. Joy and suffering struggled within him and he
was elevated in his powerlessness, sad and joyful at the same

time. He was seldom at such a loss as when he felt the pain in his hands and feet. Francis was beside himself. In every fiber of his body he experienced the event, which he so completely identified with. When a brother saw his feet later and asked what it was, Francis answered him, *Take care of what concerns you.*

> ***Francis:*** *I certainly know why I wanted to keep my experience on La Verna to myself. There's nothing evil wants more than to blacken purity, and the overly pious, who wear purity on their sleeve, don't cause any less harm. Not only today do we live in a world of voyeurism. Nothing is personal or private anymore, and everything is dragged through the mud in public view. The more the essential disappears, the more we feed on the banal or sensational. Whether my stigmata was real or not interested a lot of people, and in the same way the pious imagined they would get to heaven faster because they believed in the stigmata.*
>
> *Instead of facing their own lives, some would rather nose around in other people's private business. Religion and the church seem to be especially susceptible. People look for an excuse. They grab on to everything that distracts them from having to look at themselves in the mirror. It's always the others who are forced to justify their own lives. The decisive questions are not asked anymore. Instead, we feed on the scandals of others. But the questions remain for the voyeur as well as for the pious, regardless of how hard they try to repress them: How do you live yourself? Who do you serve? What are your values? And how successful are you at living them? A lot of things would be very different if we would first take care of what concerns us, if we would first take hold of ourselves. This is the core of spiritual truthfulness.*

The Song of Brother Sun

In his thoughts Francis was free, humble and passionate at the same time. His body, however, plagued him more and more. Brother Ass was the part of him who was taking a rapid turn for the worse. In part he had himself to blame—owing to the overexertion of his body and the illnesses from the journey to the East. His nights were getting darker and the days resembled more and more the nights. Whatever he tried became increasingly difficult and just dealing with the pain cost him much of his strength. Body and spirit struggled with each other. One had wished and hoped with all its passion, while the other could not go on and saw, with suffering and tolerance, the end coming nearer. Movements were becoming more painful and Francis could only see when the tears and pus in his eyes allowed him to. He had never worried about his body, but now it was catching up to him. It not only put limitations on him but now forced him, as never before, to take his physical existence seriously.

In the spring of 1225, his eye illness not only worsened but his entire physical condition did so as well. The cardinal protector increasingly pressed him to get an eye operation, and Brother Elias, to whom he had sworn obedience, supported the cardinal. It will do no good if you don't let yourself be helped, the cardinal said. Francis' health was important to him and to the brothers, and if he didn't see it that way and thought he had to remain tough then he would have to be forced to get help. Francis journeyed to the Rieti Valley, where the best doctors of the Roman Curia would be sent to treat him. Despite the best doctors and the best intentions of his supporters, in the end the treatment still proved to be a medical martyrdom.

In the spring of 1223, the forty-three-year-old Francis made his way to the Rieti Valley with several of his closest brothers. The doctors had not yet arrived, and it was very cold this time of year. The weather was not conducive to his cure. The brothers found shelter with a poor country priest in whose lowly dwelling they were given a soot-darkened room where they cooked, ate and slept. They held the Liturgy of the Hours in the adjoining old chapel. Below the house was a little grotto with a cleft in the rocks they covered with straw. Francis found shelter there. But this time it was not a refuge he withdrew to by choice. He could simply no longer bear the light of day nor the smoke in the communal room.

Day and night his eyes were in such great pain that he could hardly rest or sleep. When he fell asleep the mice, who were more than at home in this forgotten shelter, woke him. During these days Francis suffered indescribably, and it was not unusual that self-pity overcame him. He turned to God and again had a dream, a vision or both at the same time. This was nothing new for Francis and it had always functioned before—not on demand but through his openness. Constantly he repeated a verse of a psalm that voiced his plea: *Lord, hasten to help me.*

The answer first came to him like a code: *Imagine that instead of your illness someone gave you a treasure that was more valuable than all the gold on earth. Wouldn't that make you happy?* It was as if Francis were outside himself, yet at the same time completely one with his inner core. Now everything was at stake. What could he still do? What could he be capable of? What could still be possible in a life that had reached its physical end? A new momentum could not be reckoned with anymore, or could it? Of course it's over, it would be deception to think anything else. The treasure was a different one. Maybe it was a clear dream or a vision in the long nights. The message Francis received was unmistakably clear: *You can feel as safe as if you were already in my kingdom.*

Possibly nothing had made him so happy in his whole life. As pitifully as he crouched in his cleft in the rock, he sang and rejoiced inwardly. He felt his suffering and at the same time felt strong—undefeatable, as the knight of the past would have said. Thankfulness toward God and all his creation flowed through his hurting body. He wanted to sing and, in his dark hole, suddenly thought of creation, of his beloved nature that he could barely see anymore, of the sun and the stars and the moon that shone down on him so often in the hours of night. What he felt inside overflowed. He leaned back, the melody was there and the first words came: *Exalted, almighty, good Lord.* Francis suffered and composed, forgetting himself more and more.

He sang in the way he had always wished for his brothers: not only to preach but also to sing praises to the Lord. He sang, as he had always done when he was well and broke into the song of the troubadours. He sang in the way he had always believed was right for his brothers and himself as minstrels of the Lord. He sang because he had always wanted to move the hearts of people and he sang simply because of his longing to sing. He began: *Exalted, almighty, good Lord, yours is the praise, the glory and the honor and every grace. They belong to you alone, and no one is worthy to speak your name.*

Francis sat in the dark grotto because he could no longer bear the light, but his thoughts were of day and night. He could hardly experience them anymore physically, but all the more did they appear before him. God should be praised every morning, he thought, because he created the day, and in the same way at night because of the moon and the fire that brightens the night.

Where would we be without them? Francis leaned back once more and the melody was there again, and with it the words: *Praise be to you my Lord, in all your creation, especially Brother Sun, as he creates the day and gives us light through you. And he is beautiful and radiant in his splendor. He proclaims you, exalted Lord. Praise be to you, my Lord for Sister Moon and the stars. You have formed them in the heavens, bright shining, precious and beautiful. Praise be to you my Lord in Brother Fire, through whom you illuminate the night; he is handsome, worthy of love, powerful and strong.*

Francis no longer felt any pain. He was no longer in himself but in nature, inside God's creation, in the place where he had always felt at home and close to his self. And he did not sing in an idyllic place, but behind the darkness of his eyes and on a night when he was close to despair. But again he had received an answer—an assurance—and now it was decisive. His song was not shallow sentiments about nature but the answer to the promise he had just been given. Francis thanked his Creator, and no thanks could have been more heartfelt. In one of the darkest nights a person could live through, tormented by illness and suffering, he was certain of his deliverance. He leaned back once more and the melody was there again. He was outside and saw the heavens and wind, everything he would never sense this way again; and he sang in the darkness of his cell: *Praise be to you, my Lord, in Brother Wind and through the air and clouds and clear sky and every weather which sustains your creation. Praise be to you, my Lord, through Sister Water, for she is so useful and humble, precious and pure.* The water running through his shelter flowed within him. He sat in the dark womb of Mother Earth and sang: *Praise be to you, my Lord, in our*

Sister Mother Earth, who nourishes and guides us and brings forth a bounty of fruit and bright flowers and herbs.

The Canticle of the Creatures, sometimes called *The Canticle of Brother Sun,* was created at the end of his life in the light of deliverance. It gave voice to anticipated jubilation and at the same time was great comfort in his illness. Again and again he sang the verses, and the worse his physical suffering became the more often and the more fervently he sang. He could forget his pain when he sang. The singing of his song, the waves of the melody and rhythm and his immersion in the essence of the verse carried him to another place. Francis put himself in the setting of God's creation, felt connected with all of its beings and joined in their praise of the Lord. It helped. Later, when he was no longer able to sing, he often had his brothers sing the song of Brother Sun to him. It helped because rather than being cheap consolation, Francis sang the song in the certainty of his redemption. It helped because the song was not just a sentimental distraction, but in fact an expression of the attitude he had always lived. Whenever Francis washed his hands he chose a place where the water could run off into the earth again. When he wandered over the rocks, he did it with reverence for the stone under his feet. He had told Brother Gardener not just to plant edible herbs in the garden but to save a section of the earth for the other kind as well. And he should also plant herbs and flowers just for the sake of their fragrance and beauty. He seemed to speak to the birds, and once in a while a rabbit from the field ventured near him, or even let him pet it. Francis was connected to nature, the creation of God, in a special way, and in these dark hours, while he sang the praise of Brother Sun he was one with it.

Francis*: Brother Sun and Sister Moon and Mother Earth were, for me, as real as could be. At this time, when I was already very sick, and could hardly see anymore, I often thought back to the little woods near the Portiuncula, the marshy landscapes below my home-town, the waving wheat fields of Rivotorto, the gentle hills near Bevagna in the spring on the other side of the Spoleto Valley. The birds and insects always gave a never-ending concert of peeping, whistling and hum-ming, and I was right in the middle of it. I didn't preach to them, but they preached to me. It seemed to me as if they were constantly talking about their Creator. How often did I take a walk in the little woods near the Portiuncula. It was, if I could just be sentimental for a minute, a stroll in the middle of God's creation. I was startled every time a twig broke under my feet. I enjoyed the silence, walked slower and slower, sometimes stop-ping to lean against a tree and blink up into the sunlight. I welcomed every ant crawling across my neck or on my finger. I could watch their actions for hours on end, and this always had a calming effect on me. When I was alone in nature like that, it always transformed me. I hummed with the bees and whistled with the birds. I often caught myself standing for a long time next to a tree and smiling for no reason.*

The brothers said that I would always act complete-ly crazy when I returned from such walks. They must have sensed how good nature was for me. I felt one with everything—with God and with myself. I was in balance. Sometimes when I was anxious or things got to be too much for me, and I didn't know what to do, I withdrew alone in nature, to my other brothers and sisters. There I soon found again the way to my inner peace. At night the stones, leaves and moss were transformed by the moon and shimmered with indescribable radiance. The view of the wide heavens with its many stars filled me with a deep thankfulness every time. From time to time I got up on a tree or a little hill to really be able to feel the wind. It helped me again and again to blow many things away. Nature is available for you, but especially you men need to remember that it doesn't have to do with sport or per-formance, but with letting go and coming home.

At one time or another I also became sad at these moments. Then I sensed that there was something I was pushing away from myself. Sometimes tears ran down my face, the rain that comes from inside and cleanses in the same way as the wind and weather. Sometimes I also looked for the challenge—maybe I wanted to test my lim-itations. It was those days and nights in caves, on rock slabs or under a rocky overhang. It was the less idyllic seasons, the rain and the cold, the hard rocks, the rolling of the thunder, the darkness, storms and bad weather. At these times I had to tolerate a lot until I was one with them again, until I could once more embrace these harsher brothers and sisters. But they belonged to me and I to them.

Francis still cowered in his narrow grotto. The cycle of the canticle drew to its end and the singer arrived at his own self. He had never thought much about Brother Ass, and he sat, out of necessity, in a dark hole, yet filled with certainty and praise for the Lord in his creation. Things were as they were and there was no turning back. But first the acid test with Brother Fire was before him. When it was time for his eyes to be treated, the brothers brought him to the other side of the Rieti Valley to Fonte Colombo, the hermitage where he had composed the final Rule two years earlier. He pulled the hood over his head and the brothers bandaged his eyes with an additional cloth. The pain was so great that he could no longer stand daylight. They brought him by horseback to the other side of the valley. He would normally have refused such a luxury if he had been in a condition to put one foot in front of the other. But now everything was different. A doctor was waiting for him there who was considered a specialist for illnesses of the eyes.

He explained to Francis what he was going to do. The doctor said that to his best knowledge the water and pus, which continually ran from Francis' eyes, came from canals above his temples. For this reason he would have to burn out these canals, from his ears over his cheeks, up to his brows so that the flow would be stopped. It sounded horrible and Francis hesitated. He was afraid. He wanted to delay the operation until Brother Elias and the minister general had arrived. Elias had ordered the operation, together with the cardinal, and the brothers waited daily for the arrival of the order superior. Francis waited, too, but the superior did not come. At some point the news arrived that he was held up by numerous obligations. Francis and the three

or four brothers who waited with him were alone with what lay
before him and them. Those who had ordered it were themselves
not present. They were all afraid of what was to come. It was,
however, not only obedience, but also the condition itself that
compelled Francis to submit to this terrible procedure. They
only knew later that it was useless and did not bring relief, something we see from our perspective today. Following a night when
Francis could not sleep because of his pain, he called his brothers to him. He sensed their worry and even more the fear in their
pale faces staring at him, unable to utter a word. For weeks and
months they had been with him, undergone sacrifice and never
left his side. Francis wanted to raise their spirits, to give them
courage and would gladly have given back to them what they had
summoned up for him. Powerless and at the same time filled
with faith, he lifted himself up a little. *I am the little servant of
God,* he said to them in a broken voice, *and God will give back
to you what you have done for me.* When the time came the
brothers fled anyway. They simply could not witness it. The doctor came and brought the iron used to carry out the cauterizing
of his temples, as it was called in those days. He had a fire made
to heat the iron, and laid the instrument in it. Francis saw the
fire and his song was there again: *Praise be to you, my Lord, in
Brother Fire, through whom you illuminate the night; he is
handsome, worthy of love, powerful and strong.* He sang the
same verse over and over again. Then he addressed Brother Fire
directly: *Be friendly to me in this hour,* and he made the Sign of
the Cross over the fire. The doctor began with the burning and
Francis embraced Brother Fire.

Almost boisterously, he called to his brothers, who after some
time cautiously peeked inside, *You, fainthearted ones, I felt no
pain nor the heat of the fire.* The doctor was no less surprised

because he had never experienced anything like this before. Francis had not even moved, but still it had done no good. So much was certain, later, when the wounds were partially healed, his eyes were still in pain, they still watered and he could see even less than before. When he could be moved in the spring, he was brought by order to the heights above Siena, where another specialist carried out a further senseless procedure. The clever ones meant well with him. He had to endure these procedures and the brothers who were closest to him had to witness them.

Still in Siena six months before his death, his whole condition worsened. It was much more than his eyes that hurt him. Because of his constant illness and an additional liver problem, his stomach failed him. He threw up blood, and it was clear to the brothers that he would not live much longer. This time Brother Elias reacted personally. In the early summer of 1226, the minister general brought Francis, who was then forty-four, from Siena to the hermitage Celle di Cortona. Here he stayed for a while, before he was brought back to Assisi at his own request. His body was swollen and his legs, feet and stomach failed him more and more. He could hardly take in any nourishment.

Francis sensed that his days were coming to an end, but his spirit was still full of vitality. The brothers with him were among his closest confidants. Most of them were the brothers of the first hour, simple and true men, for whom it only had to do with Francis and living according to the Scriptures he had lived out for them. Even if he could no longer see, he was not blind. What was happening in his order in the meantime did not remain hidden from his view. It was reported to him how his Rule was discussed by the brothers and examined by the "senior brains," how a multitude of powers and interpretations had evolved from the simplicity of the order founders. Still once more he thought back to the beginning and again he wanted to raise his voice, to leave something behind for all time.

In the seclusion and quiet of Celle di Cortona, where only a little creek splashed under the narrow cell, he dictated his *Testament* to a fellow brother. His thoughts recalled the day when it had all begun: *And then when I departed from the leper, it was as if everything bitter was transformed into a sweetness of the soul and the body,* he dictated. His sentences mostly began with "and": *And after the Lord gave me brothers, no one showed me what I had to do, rather the Highest himself had revealed to me I was to live according to the directive of the Holy Scriptures.* He described the modest happiness of the brothers in this first period: *And they were satisfied with robes patched on the inside and outside, including a rope belt and pants. And we did not want anything more.*

Once more he repeated the themes dearest to him, so as to emphasize their importance to his brothers. At the same time, he stressed the Rule, the form of life that was to remain unshakable. Francis sensed what was at stake: *And the Minister General and all the other ministers are held to obedience not to add anything to my words or to take anything from them. And they should always have my testament with them as well as the Rule.* In conclusion he gave them his blessing. However, it was too late, not for his blessing but for *The Testament.* Three years after his death, the cardinal protectorate himself, at that time Pope Gregory IX, annulled the validity of *The Testament* with pressure from the order superiors. The development could no longer not be halted, even if Francis had tried one more time.

Francis: I tried again, but in reality it was a farewell. As weighty as it sounds, I was actually saying goodbye to my life and my task in the words I dictated. The part about letting go sounds so easy. Maybe I even succeeded in making what I dictated not sound like a letting go. And then I didn't want to weigh it down with my death, so I remained silent about that.

You live your life, make your mark in it and leave traces of yourself behind. Then they take on their own life. You fight back and make corrections. For a while you still count; they still listen to you. You have your wedding festivals—times when everything goes as you dreamt it should. You are happy and enthusiastic. The mistake is that you think it will always stay this way. One day you have to come to terms with the fact that things have continued without you, that your opinion isn't asked for anymore, even for something that's got your name on it. You notice that your life is a curve, not an upward soaring line, and you notice at some point that your voice is no longer being heard. And it keeps on this way until one day you feel the curve is reaching its end. But letting go has a dimension that continues into eternity, otherwise we would keep hanging on to it.

Maybe my Testament was so vehement because I was thinking about the directive the Lord had given to us. Some of the developments in the order preoccupied me more than my own death, which I could sense coming. Don't take yourself so seriously, I always told myself, and yet the matter I had spent my whole life on was so important to me. I was continually tossed back and forth. I could find no solution. I first found peace when I found the place where I fit at the end of my life, when I could inwardly accept that I was reaching my end, and things are as they are, that they will be as they will be. And in this way I reached the maturity to die.

BROTHER DEATH

Francis wanted to return to the Portiuncula to die. Because of the oppressive summer heat, he was first brought to Bagnaia, in the cool mountains above Assisi. It seemed as if the vultures were already waiting. Even now they had their eye on the relics. In Assisi they were already thinking about what should be done after some brothers had attempted to get hold of small remnants of his robe as keepsakes. The city was still in constant rivalry with its neighbor Perugia, and when a renewed worsening of his condition was reported, the city fathers feared the neighbors might be quicker and kidnap the future saint. Soldiers were sent as quickly as possible to Bagnaia to bring him to the city under military escort, to the bishop's palace where he could be better cared for.

Francis directed the personal circumstances surrounding his death as was befitting him, with gestures and rituals, as well as he still could. In the bishop's palace he had all the brothers from the Portiuncula assemble and blessed each of them individually. He had to touch each head in his blindness and his hand found Brother Elias, whom he blessed in a special way. There was no word of criticism or warning. *May God remember your efforts and work,* he said to his successor in his office and he knew what he was talking about. Afterward he asked for Brother Bernard, the first of his brothers, who at that time had divided all of his possessions among the poor, and recommended him as a special role model for the other brothers. Elias was the man of action, in whose hands the responsibility for the order was placed, and in Bernard Francis saw himself reflected. In these blessings he balanced charisma with the leader and the realm of what was possible with the ideal.

The final hour was inevitably approaching and Francis had himself taken to the Portiuncula for the last time, on the way stopping to say goodbye to his hometown of Assisi in a blessing. He had two of his brothers sing the *Canticle of the Creatures* one last time, including the verse he had added in the last few weeks: *Praise be to you, my Lord, through our Sister bodily death; for no man can escape her.* He had someone bring him bread, which he blessed, broke and gave to his brothers. He used the celebration of the Last Supper as a ritual to say goodbye to his brothers. At the same time one of them read aloud the passage from Scripture.

An unexpected and at the same time touching moment occurred in the last hours before his death. The great ascetic asked once more for his favorite pastry. The woman should be called with whose family he had, upon occasion, been a guest. She should bring an ash-gray cloth for his body, a small linen cloth for his face, candles, a pillow and the cakes that he had always liked to eat so much. As if she had already sensed what was to come, Brother Jacopa, as he had sometimes affectionately called her, was there at once with the items for which he had asked.

On the evening of October 3, 1226—a Saturday evening— Francis died at the Portiuncula. From the nearby woods the lark was heard singing. This was the bird that had always been his favorite. Sister Lark was very close to him because she, too, searched for her food on the street and, if she had to, even searched in the dung of animals to find a piece of straw. He loved her especially because of her unpretentious gray, speckled plumage and the little hood on her head, which reminded him of his own. Sister Lark was the color of the earth that he now lay on. Francis finally embraced his Brother Death as he had wished, naked on the naked ground. He had asked the brothers to leave him this way as long as was needed to walk the distance of one mile without hurry.

Francis: My hour had come—one that you would rather forget. What should I say about death? For many of you death is an opponent and you live your life doing battle with it. You repress what is part of your life, or will unavoidably be so, probably because you believe that afterward everything will be different. But death is our brother—or sister, as I said in the Canticle—who brings to an end what has come to an end. He takes us out of this life, to give us over to a new life. He knows how much in us isn't finished, and still hasn't been brought to an end, and in fact doesn't draw a final line below our life. He accompanies us in the transition, so that there can be good in what wasn't before.

He is a gentle brother, even when we are so afraid of him. We rebel, fight one more time, struggle and don't want to admit that he's real. I lived through that myself in the months before my death. We fight and grapple with him, and when we are lying in his arms still resist. In the end he costs us all our strength. Then the moment comes, even when it's very short, when we surrender to him and to our life. Suddenly it's a relief not to struggle, not to have to fight anymore. Then we are ready to give our-selves up into his arms. It is a warm and light feeling when he receives us. Brother Death is good to us when he takes us with him. There's not much more I can tell you about dying.

Brother Death could help you men to see life in a kinder way. He doesn't make everything senseless, but he can teach you the differences between what is essential and nonessential, what is unimportant and the human side of life, what is transient and momentary and what remains in the end. You see your life differently when you look at it from the perspective of the eternal. But you probably don't have any time for this.

Brother Death could teach you what success is: standing firm, facing the realities and challenges of life, being flexible without betraying your own self, being compatible without denying who you are, remaining true to your values—outwardly and inwardly—and living out what you have chosen. True success isn't measured in moments. It also has to be able to stand up against your Brother Death. This is what fills up your life when you are then prepared to give yourself up to him. Today you like to push Brother Death away from you and don't want to hear anything about him. Eternal life, eternal youth and eternal potency are the ridiculous mottos professed by their advocates, who, incidentally, die earlier than they might due to stress. When you deny death, he will pursue you from behind and then you become the one on the run. Then life becomes your last chance, because you believe that afterward it will all come to an end, and you must pack everything you possibly can into it. In essence life then becomes a nightmare. It's like the speck of dust that sits in the groove of a record—for those of you who remember records. The turntable suddenly starts to turn and the needle is placed on the record. The speck of dust can only go forward, faster and faster inescapably, and there is no way of knowing after which curve the needle will catch up to it. When you repress death you will also live your life out of breath like this.

Every enjoyment becomes a source of stress, because you never know when it will be the last. Your life only revolves around extending this time and the question of what you can cram into it. In doing so you are actually running away from what could make the difference in your life. This has nothing more to do with true enjoyment. I'm probably not exactly an expert on enjoyment, but I can tell you this much: you will be able to truly enjoy when you believe that everything's not over with death, when you are lifted up by the confidence that life continues. Only then can you first truly enjoy, because then you have a taste of what's to come. What else can I tell you? You can take what I've said seriously or not. You can take yourself seriously or not. You can continue just to exist or not. Or you can also take some down time, listen inside yourself and ask yourself the important questions. Death is your brother and he wants to be near to you for a long time. His question would be: What would you do if you only had four months to live? He gives you more, but he asks you the question. Your life begins with you. And most importantly: There is something you can do.

Francis for Men: A Spiritual Mystery Tour

Men think differently, or so it seems. Theology speaks about faith as the *mysterium fascinosum et tremendum* ("fascinating and frightening mystery"). Here, on one hand the fascination of life is at the forefront, the wonder of life itself, such as the wonder of love between two people and the love of God, but at the same time there exists here the frightening and mysterious as well, such as death and suffering, and our daily experience of limitations and deficiencies. Maybe it's a characteristic of male spirituality that these two poles stand in a fruitful tension to one another. The frightening part of faith, the *tremendum*, resists every form of prettied-up piety.

In depictions of Francis of Assisi the *tremendum*—the mysterious and the wild—is often repressed. Thus Francis is represented alternatively as either the stuffy man of piety or the environmentalist nature-saint. The secluded places of his hermitages alone put a scratch on this picture. They are not easily accessible, charming, idyllic settings. They are sometimes mysterious, if not even frightening, and yet they convey something that cannot be put into words. Spirituality, perhaps specifically spirituality for men, is sometimes almost tangible here.

A Male Journey of Spirituality

Men believe in a different way and often don't themselves know how they believe. Perhaps the fact that they are seekers is a part of this. Therefore, what could be more fitting than to set out with others on a search, going part of the spiritual way together. I have been the director of the Office for Men's Issues and Questions at the Catholic church in Voralberg, Austria, for several years, so what could be more natural for me than to take a pilgrim journey with men to visit just these places? Our guide should be less the idealized Francis, the saint with the pious expression, and much more Francis the energetic man with the strong inner ideals and the relentless will to accomplish what he set out to do.

Imagine grown men praying with each other outdoors, dancing in a circle, singing evening Vespers—in three-part harmony—at the end of the journey. Can today's men do this? Yes, they can. Twelve men, who couldn't have been more different, set out together during a week in May on an adventurous journey. They were a politician, a trucker, an electrician, an architect, a publisher, a technician, a young pensioner, an adult educator, a personnel advisor, a civil engineer and a consultant for men's issues. We met as strangers and a week later went our separate ways as brothers. To quote from some of the writing by the men during that week,

> *Men with totally different professions and backgrounds, each with his own unique story, came together for only a few days in a way that I had never experienced.*

When men open themselves up to each other there is an undeniable feeling of adventure present.

> *When I think back on it, on how I freed myself from the shell of the all-knowing and powerful and opened myself to the unknown dynamic of a group, I sense again this unique tension unknown until now: a tension on the razor's edge between fear and joy.*

On a weeklong round-trip journey through central Italy in three campers, we followed the footsteps of Francis. It was not the town of Assisi that was the focus, but instead the secluded hermitages, impressive places far from the world, in the middle of nature, on rough rocks, quiet and almost mysterious. Here loneliness and silence stand in fruitful tension to a clear perspective of the world. Francis of Assisi was not a hermit, but he retreated again and again to such places for periods of time, to reflect on the essential, to refill his inner well of strength and to be close to God. It is a model that is also healing for us men: "In the future I need more room for myself, my own little hermitages in time and place. I want to create them for myself and need them for my positive energies to grow—for my life as a husband, father, friend, godfather, colleague—simply as a man."

The monastic form of liturgical prayer, Lauds and Vespers, as well as times of silence were a part of our journey, as was dialogue, singing and dancing. Likewise, time was devoted to celebration together. In the afternoon we found a place to stop for a snack, and then let daytime flow into evening with a shared meal at an Italian *trattoria*. He who is not able to laugh, cry, sing, pray, eat, drink. . . is also not able intrinsically to believe. Spirituality needs flesh and blood. It was all a single element, each part as self-evident as the other and the whole expressed in a brotherly community of men: "At the beginning I had conflicting feelings. But then I became more and more curious, even hungry for new male experiences. In the end, not one was unpleasant among them. Whether it was the dance, prayer, song or the very personal dialogues, I wouldn't have wanted to miss any of it—on the contrary, I want even more."

A member of the group thanked his fellow brothers with the following words:

> I've gained a lot for my life through our shared pilgrim trip, a new dimension, one that has been sleeping inside me for a long time, waiting to be activated. Especially the daily prayer with all of you—after I got over my inner resistance—thinking how in the

*world I was going to pray two times a day, and then
finding out just how important this inner peace was
twice a day. Your sometimes sleepy, sometimes overly loud, mostly calming, reverent, male voices
remind me of my connection with you in a personal
area—my male spirituality. Almost daily I found a
sentence in one of our prayers that moved me and
seemed to be directed at me personally. There was
no question that it left a deep impression on me to
stand in a circle with eleven like-minded men, to
pray and to sing, and have the chance to sense the
manly energy we expressed.*

The Mysterious Places

The hermitages where Francis often withdrew for weeks at a
time in prayer and contemplation resist every form of prettied-
up spirituality. In Celle di Cortona we found the first contact
with this reality of Francis of Assisi, and it was an ideal place to
collect ourselves for the first time inwardly. The drive there
takes you over a slope through woods and olive fields. In the distance you see only what looks like a stone quarry until you get
closer and an old monastery takes shape out of the rocks. An
excerpt from the journal we kept describes the atmosphere:

*The steep brook rushing through the middle reaches
to the soul. I encounter a feeling of timelessness, or
better yet, everything in the present, the warmth of
the sun, the freshness of the rushing water, the stony
quiet of the cells . . . In the dormitorium, where
Francis' cell is located, the door is first open and
sunshine streams warmly inside the cool, but also
the disturbing noise of other visitors. Without giving
it any thought I close the door, and we then have the
chance to collect our thoughts in the quiet—this*

> *could be the recipe for my daily life as well—close*
> *the door—and then I can come to the oasis of quiet*
> *when things get hectic.*

Quiet and silence were called for when we visited these places,
even when the other people on a Sunday outing didn't always
share this feeling. But at some point we were alone again:

> *Spending a long time in these places, just being*
> *quiet, really affected me deeply. To spend five or ten*
> *minutes in absolute silence in a place where Francis*
> *had prayed eight hundred years ago was a powerful*
> *experience for me. But the quiet especially meant for*
> *me just listening. It could be really difficult at times,*
> *but something inside me was moved by it.*

One of the most impressive places was the hermitage Lo Speco.
Indeed the familiar characteristics of a Franciscan hermitage are
found here in an incomparably unspoiled state. Lo Speco has
retained these, due in large part to its considerable degree of iso-
lation. Above the small monastery the rock reveals a long crack,
leading approximately sixty-five yards inside the mountain. It is
the same grotto where Francis himself withdrew for prayer and
meditation. The brothers of the little monastery compare the
opening in the rock with the rocks that split open in the hour of
Christ's death: *the earth quaked and the rocks split open.* Just
how little this has to do with religious romanticism becomes
even more evident after one of our group actually dares to venture deeper inside. He barely spoke about what he experienced
inside this opening in the rock the rest of the week. We first gain
an understanding in his written description:

> *As we stood in front of it, I had a feeling that I would*
> *be able to gain contact with the hard reality Francis*
> *experienced here in a special way—if I had the*

nerve to go inside. This decision was one I made, more or less easily, but when I set off after breakfast—armed with a miner's hard hat and a parka—I had a feeling of excitement and tension and, although it was a warm day, felt a chill pass through me upon entering.

Inside, I was first in the roomy lit area, then the very narrow passageway slanting down into the earth. The lamp only served as a means of initial orientation, then I had to force myself through, sliding along step by step—there was at least only one way to go—I caught myself on the sharp corners and made my way past damp stone slabs and walls, loose places on the wall and ghostly shadows. I could feel my heart, which seemed to have slipped down somewhere inside me, thumping in my brain. Again and again I took a break to catch my breath, although it wasn't physically strenuous. I then turned off the lamp: the darkness was heavy and it seemed as if I could almost take hold of it—absolute silence—both seemed to weigh on me. The single sound of a drop of water somewhere in the distance was incredibly loud. I asked myself: What if there are animals in here?—I was blocking the opening completely with my body . . . On a rock ledge slanting over my face I suddenly noticed a large spider—I almost sensed relief at the sight of this creature (spiders are pets at my house). I could hardly make out where the place I came to was leading, despite the lamp. After a few deep breaths, half lying down, I pushed myself forward feeling the way down below with my feet, always trying alternatives, in my mind afraid of getting stuck. But what if one of the pieces *of stone from above should come loose? In this moment I couldn't imagine how it would be possible to get me out . . . To calm myself I started to pray and sing the* Canticle of the Creatures *in the original version Francis composed. Francis was in here so often and for such long periods of time. I could easily imagine that hallucinations would be possible during longer stays inside here.*

I probably didn't trust myself to enter the last narrow space. I saw a little place where it was possible to lie down and, raised slightly at the end, a little hollow to sit on. I now also felt a certain awkwardness, as if I was intruding on a private or holy place. The air was noticeably fresh and damp, without any trace of moldiness. I remained in this darkness for a long time. I sensed the rock around me, completely surrounding me, intense and mysterious at the same time. I am moved to my inner core. The moisture penetrates my bones, along with fear that the earth, the rock could crush me, swallow me, and still there is also the feeling of home, tenderness—and most of all nothing else seems as important to me at this moment as giving myself up to this turmoil of feelings.

A certain chill remained with me for days after, and especially at the damp rock clefts of La Verna it was completely there again. Also now, while writing, the feeling from that time can be sensed again, and this deep, stirring experience is a true gift.

In Poggio Bostone, high above on a rock, Francis found the reconciliation with his past he had come there for and, consequently, saw his future clearly before him. We twelve men followed this way, each for himself and each with his own past:

> *Although I am an experienced mountain climber I*
> *had more trouble on this comfortable, half-hour hike*
> *than on one of my usual mountain climbing trips. It*
> *was probably the themes of "letting-go of my past*
> *and hurt" that made me sweat.*

We left some things there above, hurt, shame and old wounds. We
burned some of the sick feelings at the end in the fire:

> *In the hermitage Poggio Bostone I gave my pride and*
> *impatience to the fire. I fear the flames haven't burned*
> *up everything. There still remains much to do.*

At this time we also experienced how reconciliation with the
past gives us strength for the future:

> *The meditation in front of Francis' cave in Poggio*
> *Bostone remains unforgettable for me. I sat on the*
> *smooth rock face surrounded by trees. Only a nar-*
> *row view into the wide remote valley was visible. I*
> *felt protected and I meditated. I felt the strength of*
> *the earth and held my inner vision clearly directed*
> *forward to be able to recognize what was new.*

Brotherly Care

Francis had composed a separate Rule for the hermitages where
only three to four brothers stayed at a time. In the beginning in
uncharacteristically sensitive images he describes the form of
life the brothers should share in the hermitage and in doing this
he uses the New Testament story of Martha and Mary. *They*
should live together, he also writes, *as a mother and son: one*
in contemplation, the other caring for the needs of the other.
After a certain time the duties and roles would then be reversed.
This Rule also applied to our journey, where we changed parts
each day, meaning two men at a time were the active ones and
caregivers (the Marthas) for a day, while the other two let themselves be looked after: whether this meant letting themselves be

driven somewhere, letting someone else take care of gas and water, buying provisions, setting and clearing the table or doing the dishes. It was a very unusual but good experience for a man to be able to care for another man, and for a man to be taken care of by other men. I would like consciously to claim this for myself as a male element instead of calling it the female dimension of a man. We can, as men, be attentive, caring, loving, concerned, fatherly, brotherly. The others experienced this in a similar way:

> *In our society I'm often struck by just how compli-*
> *cated our rules and statutes can be and how dispro-*
> *portional the standards are set for individual under-*
> *takings. How easily and harmoniously did our com-*
> *munal living take shape during these days, ordered*
> *by the Franciscan monastery rules to serve and be*
> *served. I witnessed in our group the courage to*
> *express simplicity, respect and appreciation for*
> *partners and colleagues. Through this a happy and*
> *good-humored group developed in these few days.*

Something Happened

In my life I have come in contact with a wide range of spiritual offerings. More than a few were good and nice—maybe offering a chance to recharge my batteries—but when it came right down to it, they didn't penetrate very deeply. In the spiritual retreat I have described above, we did more than just talk, and that was good. We did something and because of that something happened inside us. This can clearly be seen in the reactions of the participants:

> *After this spiritual week I feel like a gassed-up jet*
> *ready to take off again into the territory of "adver-*
> *sarial life."*

> *Today I'm glad I took part in this trip. Through it*
> *unimagined possibilities have been opened to me.*

The most important experience of the week was the motivation to focus again on what's essential in my life. And not only to be aware of it but also to show it.

Through our pilgrimage my life has taken on a new dimension, one that slumbered in me for a long time and was waiting to be activated.

All of this turned the tour into a focal point, a milestone, in my life.

What I'm taking with me is the knowledge of the tension I'm actually living in. What I mean by that is the tension between my inner wish for simplicity on one hand, and on the other hand the always more complicated and networked way of thinking and working in our society. That's something I'll just have to live with for the time being. Francis showed me a very uncompromising way.

The encounter with the radicalism and endearing simplicity of the otherwise so often kitsch-laden image of Francis became an inner resource that continues to work inside me like leaven and now in the weeks following has seasoned my life and given it depth. That's something I want to keep on nurturing.

None of us came back the same as before we left. Something happened that week that affected our lives and will continue to affect it. And maybe that was exactly the Franciscan part of this week. Francis didn't make lengthy speeches with a lot of nice words. He listened inside himself and changed his life, and in his case he turned it upside down. He did something after something happened inside him.

FRANCISCAN RESOURCES AVAILABLE FROM ST. ANTHONY MESSENGER PRESS

Books

The Almond Tree Speaks: New and Selected Writing 1974–1994, Murray Bodo (B2376)

The Autumn of Saint Francis of Assisi: Companions of Saint Francis of Assisi, Roderic Petrie, O.F.M. (B3054)

Brother Angelo Returns to Assisi: Companions of Saint Francis of Assisi, Roderic Petrie, O.F.M. (B4484)

Brother Leo Remembers Francis: Companions of Saint Francis of Assisi, Roderic Petrie, O.F.M. (B3658)

Canticle of Brother Sun, Rev. Edd Anthony, O.F.M. (9143X)

Clare: A Light in the Garden, Murray Bodo (B1221)

Clare of Assisi: Her Spirituality Revealed in Her Letters, Claire Marie Ledoux, Translated by Colette Joly Dees (B3682)

Day by Day With Followers of Francis and Clare, Pat McCloskey, O.F.M. (B3364)

Following Francis of Assisi: A Spirituality for Daily Living, Patti Normile (B2406)

The Franciscan Leader: A Modern Version of The Six Wings of the Seraph, Translated by Philip O'Mara, Franciscan Institute Publications (B1263)

Franciscan Solitude, Edited by André Cirino, O.F.M., and Josef Raischl, Franciscan Institute Publications (B0062)

Francis: The Journey and the Dream, Murray Bodo (B1167)

Francisco: El Viaje y el Sueño, Murray Bodo, translated by
Alicia Sarre, R.S.C.J. (B2058)

Francis of Assisi: Activities and Coloring Fun for Children
(B4581)

Francis of Assisi: The Message of His Writings, Thaddee
Matura, O.F.M., Translated by Paul Barrett, O.F.M CAP.,
Franciscan Institute Publications (B1271)

Francis of Assisi: The Song Goes On, Hugh Noonan, O.F.M., and
Roy Gasnick, O.F.M. (B2503)

Gospel Living: Francis of Assisi Yesterday and Today, Anton
Rotzetter, O.F.M. CAP., Willibrord-Cristian VanDijk, O.F.M. CAP.,
and Thaddee Matura, O.F.M., Franciscan Institute Publications
(B0615)

*Hope Against Darkness: The Transforming Vision of Saint
Francis in an Age of Anxiety*, Richard Rohr with John
Bookser Feister (B4859)

*The Journey into God: A Forty-Day Retreat with Bonaventure,
Francis and Clare*, Josef Raischl, S.F.O., and André Cirino,
O.F.M. (B4999)

A Retreat With Anthony of Padua: Finding Our Way, Carol
Ann Morrow (B3100)

*A Retreat With Francis and Clare of Assisi: Following Our
Pilgrim Hearts*, Murray Bodo and Susan Saint Sing (B2384)

Ritual of the Secular Franciscan Order, Benet A. Fonck, O.F.M.,
Editor (B0888)

*Saint Anthony of Padua: The Story of His Life and Popular
Devotions* (B2023)

St. Francis and the Song of Brotherhood and Sisterhood, Eric
Doyle, O.F.M., Franciscan Institute Publications (B0038)

St. Francis in San Francisco, Jack Wintz, O.F.M., Illustrated by
Kathy Baron, Paulist Press (I6844)

*Swimming in the Sun: Discovering the Lord's Prayer With
   Francis of Assisi and Thomas Merton*, Albert Haase, O.F.M.
   (B1930)
*The Sun and Moon Over Assisi: A Personal Encounter With
   Francis and Clare*, Gerard Thomas Straub (B3933)
Tales of St. Francis: Ancient Stories for Contemporary Living,
   Murray Bodo (B1957)
To Live as Francis Lived: A Guide for Secular Franciscans,
   Leonard Foley, O.F.M., Jovian Weigel, O.F.M., Patti Normile,
   S.F.O. (B3968)
*The Way of St. Francis: The Challenge of Franciscan
   Spirituality for Everyone*, Murray Bodo (B2449)
When Did I See You Hungry?, Photographed and Written by
   Gerard Thomas Straub (B5022)
The Wondrous Adventures of Saint Francis of Assisi, Tricia
   Gray (B4808)

Audio

Francis: The Journey and the Dream, Murray Bodo (A4026)
*A Retreat With Francis and Clare of Assisi: Following Our
   Pilgrim Hearts*, Murray Bodo and Susan Saint Sing (A4719)
Solanus Casey: One Man's Journey Toward Sanctity, Michael
   Crosby, O.F.M. CAP. (A6670)
To Live as Francis Lived: A Guide for Secular Franciscans,
   Leonard Foley, O.F.M., Jovian Weigel, O.F.M., Patti Normile,
   S.F.O. (A4395)

Video

*Francis and Clare of Assisi: An Account of Their
   Extraordinary Lives*, Oriente Occidente Productions
   (V3025)

Franciscan Holy Ground: Where Francis and Clare Found God, Narration and Music by John Michael Talbot, Written and Photographed by Jack Wintz, O.F.M. (V1223)

The Message of St. Francis for Today, featuring Michael Crosby, O.F.M. CAP. (V1261)

Poor Clares: A Hidden Presence, Oriente Occidente Productions (V3016)

St. Clare of Assisi, Oriente Occidente Productions (V1082)

St. Francis of Assisi, Oriente Occidente Productions (V1081)

St. Francis of Assisi: The Man Who Loved Everybody (V7130)